KU-099-554

# Democracy, Schooling
and Political Education

*Introductory Studies in Philosophy of Education*
Series Editors: PHILIP SNELDERS and COLIN WRINGE

*Education and the Value of Knowledge* by M. A. B. Degenhardt
*Can We Teach Children To Be Good?* by Roger Straughan
*Means and Ends in Education* by Brenda Cohen
*Mixed Ability Grouping: A Philosophical Perspective*
  by Charles Bailey and David Bridges
*The Education of Feeling and Emotion* by Francis Dunlop

# Democracy, Schooling and Political Education

COLIN WRINGE

*Department of Education, University of Keele*

POLYTECHNIC LIBRARY
WOLVERHAMPTON

ACC. No.
191646

CLASS

370.
115

CONTROL

DATE
-5. JUN 1995

SITE
04

WRI

London
GEORGE ALLEN & UNWIN
Boston          Sydney

© Colin Wringe, 1984.
This book is copyright under the Berne Convention. No reproduction
without permission. All rights reserved.

**George Allen & Unwin (Publishers) Ltd,**
**40 Museum Street, London WC1A 1LU, UK**

George Allen & Unwin (Publishers) Ltd,
Park Lane, Hemel Hempstead, Herts HP2 4TE, UK

Allen & Unwin, Inc.,
Fifty Cross Street, Winchester, Mass. 01890, USA

George Allen & Unwin Australia Pty Ltd,
8 Napier Street, North Sydney, NSW 2060, Australia

First published in 1984.

EDUCATION & HUMANITIES
LIBRARY
THE POLYTECHNIC
WOLVERHAMPTON

**British Library Cataloguing in Publication Data**

Wringe, C. A.
Democracy, schooling and political education. – (Introductory studies in
philosophy of education)
1. Politics and education
I. Title     II. Series
379     LC71
ISBN 0-04-370128-0
ISBN 0-04-370129-9 Pbk

**Library of Congress Cataloging in Publication Data**

Wringe, C. A. (Colin A.)
Democracy, schooling, and political education.
(Introductory studies in the philosophy of education; 6)
Bibliography: p.
Includes index.
1. Democracy. 2. Political science – Study and teaching. 3. Education – Social
aspects. 4. Self-government (in education)     I. Title.     II. Series.
JC423.W75     1984     370.11′5     84-6416
ISBN 0-04-370128-0 (alk. paper)
ISBN 0-04-370129-9 (pbk.: alk. paper)

Set in 10 on 11 point Plantin by Fotographics (Bedford) Ltd
and printed in Great Britain by Biddles Ltd, Guildford, Surrey

# Contents

# Editors' Foreword

Books that are available to students of philosophy of education may, in general, be divided into two types. There are collections of essays and articles making up a more or less random selection; and there are books which explore a single theme or argument in depth but, having been written to break new ground, are often unsuitable for general readers or those near the beginning of their course. The Introductory Studies in Philosophy of Education are intended to fill what is widely regarded as an important gap in this range.

The series aims to provide a collection of short, readable works which, besides being philosophically sound, will appeal to future and existing teachers without a previous knowledge of philosophy or philosophy of education. In planning the series account has necessarily been taken of the tendency of present-day courses to follow a more integrated and less discipline-based pattern than formerly. Account has also been taken of the fact that three- and four-year students, as well as those on shorter postgraduate and in-service courses, quite rightly expect their theoretical studies to have a clear bearing on their work in the classroom. Each book, therefore, starts from a real and widely recognised area of concern in the educational field, and explores the main philosophical approaches which illuminate and clarify it. Attention is paid to the work of both mainstream philosophers and philosophers of education. For students who wish to pursue particular questions in depth, each book contains a bibliographical essay or substantial list of suggestions for further reading. A full range of the main topics recently discussed by philosophers of education will eventually be covered by the series.

Besides having considerable experience in the teaching of philosophy of education, the majority of authors writing in the series have already received some recognition in their particular fields. In addition, therefore, to reviewing and criticising existing work, each author has his or her own positive contribution to make to further discussion.

In *Democracy, Schooling and Political Education* it is argued that teachers cannot adequately comprehend their own activity in abstraction from its social and political context. Following a brief exposition and critique of current interpretations of democracy, a number of apparent dilemmas facing the democrat in relation to schooling are examined in detail.

ix

These relate to the function of education in an unequal society, recently renewed arguments in favour of selection and private education, the government of educational institutions and the nature of the relationship between education and democracy.

Special attention is reserved for recent work in the highly contentious field of political education, a number of conflicting approaches to which are critically discussed.

Philip Snelders
Colin Wringe

# 1

# Education and Society

To many teachers and prospective teachers, talk of democracy in connection with education will provoke a reaction of impatience. The current fashion is for practical skills which will enable one to survive in the classroom. No doubt such skills are important, for without this basic equipment both our own and our pupils' time is wasted. But it is the implied contention of this book, and of others in the same series, that the obverse of the coin, impatience with all discussion of the social and political significance of our work, is misguided.

Teachers, it will be argued, cannot in the nature of things be mere operatives furnished with skills to be applied as they are directed. Their perception of the social and political context in which they do their work has an important effect on the nature of their job and the work they have to do. Their understanding of that context will necessarily influence their day-to-day activities in the classroom and make a difference both to what they teach and to how they teach it.

Perhaps one of the most obvious facts about teaching is that it is a communicating and, some would add, a controlling occupation. This is a feature which it shares with other occupations such as journalism, the law, the church and perhaps industrial and other kinds of management. These are all occupations concerned with passing on information, ideas, beliefs, instructions, with getting people to do certain things and behave in certain ways.

Such occupations may be contrasted with others, at all levels of society, which are not primarily communicating occupations. These include medicine and engineering, as well as such mundane jobs as plumbing or work in a factory. The best way of fitting an extra U-bolt or removing an appendix, or whether it is desirable to attempt these things at all, will probably be largely unaffected by whether one is in Moscow, Capetown, or New York. Any differences in what the surgeon does will largely depend on the skills and resources available, rather than on the political set-up under which the activity is performed.

1

With teaching, things are somewhat different. One might think that the best way of teaching pupils to solve quadratic equations or understand a simple text in a foreign language would be more or less universal and depend on established facts about the psychology of human learning, but even this is questionable. The way in which teachers and pupils deal with each other will reflect the relations of command and obedience prevailing and thought desirable in society generally. This in turn affects the range of teaching strategies acceptable to teachers and pupils. The mix of rote learning backed up by threat of punishment, discussion, pupil inquiry, teacher-centred and pupil-centred activity likely to be used for teaching what is ostensibly the same piece of material is not simply a matter of recognised technical efficiency, but will vary from time to time and place to place.

In particular, the extent to which it is thought permissible and desirable to encourage people to question what is said by someone in authority and the extent to which it is expected that such a person will explain and give reasons for what he says will also affect the way teachers teach, as well as the way in which pupils come to understand what they are taught.

Not only will the regime under which the teacher works affect the teaching methods he uses; it is certain to have an even more obvious influence on the content of what is taught. The authorities in most countries will be concerned that teachers should not undermine public order by subverting the assumptions and values of their particular state. Education is not simply the mindless passing on of a body of facts. Usually it is regarded as some kind of preparation for the future lives of pupils as members of their particular society. Consequently, both the beliefs and values and the information which educators are expected to transmit and give emphasis to will depend on what it is thought important for future citizens of that society to know.

Teachers are not, of course, bound to aim simply to reproduce in the next generation the society in which they currently work. Pupils have to be taught to 'cope with', to make something of, the world in which they will lead their adult lives. But such coping may not consist of enthusiastically embracing and supporting the values expressed by the society as it exists at present. It may consist of stoically grinning and bearing what cannot yet be altered, or it may consist of a determination to reform or change the current pattern of things.

The content of education reflects not only the way things are but also the way the adult generation, including teachers, think they ought to be. Teachers often aspire to make the next generation in some way better than the last. The desire to build a better – more virtuous, more powerful, juster, or in our own day simply more affluent – society often receives considerable social and official approval.

2

What the teacher sees as desirable behaviour leading to the creation of a better world may be expected to affect not only what he teaches and how he teaches it, but also how he interacts with his pupils on a minute-to-minute basis. What abilities and behaviours he and others see as important will affect not only what he lets pass and what he comments on and rebukes, but also the very terms in which such corrections and rebukes are given.

Consider, for example, the social values and assumptions implied and being instilled when some of the following remarks are made to pupils: 'It's *wicked* to waste food'; 'That's not a very *kind* thing to say to a little boy who cannot walk properly'; 'I won't have *disobedience* in my class'; 'What an *inefficient* way to put chairs away'; 'One doesn't *normally* start an essay like that, Michael'; 'Get on with it, Peter, don't be *feeble*'; 'Hurry up, *slow coach*'.

Unlike the surgeon and the plumber, the teacher cannot simply 'get on with his job' and leave social and political considerations to others. Such considerations determine in part what his job is. What he and others like him do and say in the very process of doing their job may have social and political consequences, and affect the way the next generation will see and respond to the social and political world around them.

## Education for Democracy

To bring someone up to live in a certain kind of society is not simply to pass on various views about that society and descriptions of the way it is run. To flourish or even to survive in certain kinds of society one may need certain skills, certain qualities, certain attitudes.

Readers, may be familiar with the story of a father and his son in a particular, rather tough, business community at some time in the past. In the story the father persuaded his son to climb on to a roof, supposedly to carry out some minor repair, and promptly removed the ladder. Under certain conditions, perhaps, one can simply afford to trust no one, and the father was keen to ensure that this necessary lesson was well and truly learned.

Much has been written about the kind of character and the kinds of ability and knowledge that correspond to particular sorts of society and particular sorts of political regime. One readily perceives the congruity between the qualities the father in the anecdote above was trying to pass on to his son and the demands of survival in the downtown commercial world of a busy city. Physical courage and promptness of action would obviously be desirable in a small country constantly obliged to defend itself against aggressive neighbours. Docility and obedience might be favoured in the education of subjects of an oriental despot, and so on.

3

But are there qualities of mind that are especially appropriate to a democracy? Many authors (e.g. Mill, 1861, pp. 218–27; Dewey, 1916, pp. 81–99; Mannheim, 1950, pp. 246–59) have written of the conditions under which democracy can be expected to function effectively, and some of these conditions relate to qualities of mind and character that are supposed to be necessary to democratic citizens.

In the 1960s and before, much was made of the apparent unsuitability of the content and organisation of education as it then was, and in many respects still is, for the demands of democracy and the modern world. Much of this writing (e.g. Garforth, 1962; Vaizey, 1962; Hook, 1963) now seems somewhat naïve. It was all but universally assumed that the world was rapidly changing for the better, and that Western countries could be unambiguously described as democratic. It was also more or less tacitly assumed that liberal democracy was a good thing. These assumptions formed the certainties against which prevailing practices in education were criticised.

All that was required was that education with its 'outmoded' curriculum, its authoritarian style of personal relations and its divisive organisation should be changed, so as to cease to impede the inevitable by continuing to produce the wrong sort of person. The way forward for the idealistic young teacher was clear. He would certainly meet opposition from the 'old brigade' but he had no reason to doubt either the rightness of his cause or the certainty of its eventual triumph.

Today's young teacher is probably less confident of these assumptions. It is no longer obvious that things are changing for the better, and that the most important thing is to be on the side of progress. Nor is there such a degree of consensus among well-meaning people that the Western form of democracy is genuinely democratic and unquestionably the best way for a society to arrange its affairs.

Doubts have also been expressed about the relationship in which education and democracy stand to each other. Not so long ago it was thought in a more or less uncomplicated fashion that fostering 'democratic ideals' was part of the obvious and legitimate function of education, and that education properly undertaken was bound to hasten the arrival of a truer and fuller form of democracy (see, for example, Garforth, 1962, pp. 49–68).

In contrast to this, it has more recently been asked (Scrimshaw, 1975) whether, in certain essential respects, the notions of education and democracy are not mutually contradictory, rather than conducive to each other. It has been claimed (Pring, 1975) that education essentially involves authority and (Olafson, 1973) that the relationship between teachers and pupils is necessarily an asymmetrical, that is, an unequal one. So must not education necessarily foster undemocratic attitudes? Or must not attempts to combine education with democracy be destructive of education (Cox and Dyson, 1971)? Doubts have also been raised as to whether it is even legitimate for the adult generation to attempt, through the educational system, deliberately to pass on any set of values or ideals in order to gain the commitment of the young to a particular way of life (Bereiter, 1973; Holt, 1977).

It will later be argued that some of these hesitations are misguided. For the present, however, it may be said that our society at least claims to be a democracy. Public policy, including policy in education, has to be defensible in what can be represented as democratic terms. Barring some form of military coup or other unexpected cataclysm, this is the society in which our pupils will begin their adult lives.

Some people may wish to deny that this necessarily means that teachers ought to 'educate for democracy' in the sense of trying to influence pupils in favour of democracy, or making a point of teaching such knowledge, attitudes and qualities as seem likely to help preserve our existing polity. Nevertheless, any notion of educating those who will be the future citizens of such a society must include bringing them to understand that society and to live and operate effectively within it.

It is difficult to see how a teacher could conceive, let alone pursue, such an aim if he had no understanding of what a liberal democracy purported to be. Equally he could scarcely engage in the task of educating future citizens of a democracy without giving some thought to how the presuppositions of democracy related to whatever other educational aims the teacher thought it his business to pursue.

From what has been said so far it may be thought that I am about to argue that teachers ought to be committed to 'democracy' and ought to aim to pass on something that can be called 'democratic values'. This may indeed be the conclusion we shall reach, but nothing has yet been said to commit us to any such views. The main points that have been made so far are:

(1) A teacher cannot restrict himself to the task of 'getting on with the task of teaching' without reference to the wider social and political context, for this context will have an important effect on what he has to teach and how he is able to teach it.
(2) If our society claims to be a democracy of some kind. the education of its future citizens must necessarily be concerned with enabling them to live and function in such a society and come to some understanding of it.

To say these things is a far cry from saying that our society is truly democratic, or that democracy is something of which we should approve. Even a general commitment to democracy does not entail the view that school is the place to pass on attitudes and qualities favourable to the maintenance of a democratic society. Nor does it tell us what these characteristics are or how they should be encouraged in the young.

Just what kinds of institution are democratic or appropriate to a democratic society is far from being universally agreed. Indeed, some of the bitterest and most confusing disputes in modern politics concern precisely this point. When it is claimed that such and such a politician has acted democratically or undemocratically, this is not usually an argument about what the politician has actually done, but about how the terms democratic and undemocratic are properly to be applied.

In the next chapter, therefore, I propose to begin by distinguishing between four rather different views of what democracy is and between a number of different ways in which the term democratic can be used. This is not mere pedantry, for I am not concerned with dictionary definitions or etymologies. But until we are clear about how the word democracy is being used we can make little progress on the questions of how democracy is to be justified or criticised and what role the teacher and his work have to play in a democratic society.

# 2

# The Meanings of Democracy

## Is the Word Meaningless?

It might be thought that 'democracy', rather like 'freedom', 'equality' and 'justice', is so universally approved and so universally claimed as the description of every kind of existing regime that it risks becoming totally devoid of meaning. Certainly the label is claimed by countries on both sides of the Iron Curtain, as well as by numerous states in the Third World that are neither liberal democracies nor communist regimes in the Russian mould (Macpherson, 1966).

To say, however, that the term is so widely used as to pick out no specific features whatever of the regime to which it is applied is an exaggeration. To begin with, it is an implication of describing the state as a democracy that at the very least it is supposed in some way to exist for the sake of the people in it. In this it may be contrasted with even some of the more benevolent monarchies of the past where the citizens, however well they were treated, were ultimately regarded as being there to serve their rulers, rather than vice versa. It may also be contrasted with colonial states, the interests of whose populations were often subordinate to those of the colonising power. Possibly too there may have been theocracies which saw their purpose as the service and glorification of God, or the pursuit of some other ideal extrinsic to the interests of the population. Perhaps some of the more extreme Islamic countries of the Middle East may be seen as contemporary examples of this kind of polity.

The advantage of beginning with some such very minimal condition as definitive of democracy, as we have done, enables us to recognise that both the liberal democracies of the West and the non-liberal varieties on the other side of the Iron Curtain and elsewhere are democracies of a kind. We may think that the actual regimes of East or West are tyrannical and corrupt perversions of the ideals for which they

7

claim to stand. But both kinds of state have in common that they express an ideal of a morally different kind from those in which the good of the people, whatever that good may be, is overtly subordinate to some other good or someone else's ends.

We are thereby relieved of the necessity of trying to say which brand of democracy is the 'true' one. Instead we are free to distinguish between two or more conceptions of democracy, to consider which is to be preferred, and so on, without becoming involved in disputes over definitions. Dispassionate discussion is made harder and important questions may be begged if we begin by saying that the only 'real' democracies are those of the West or those of the East or those in the Third World, and that the others only describe themselves as democracies for propaganda reasons.

## Liberal Democracies and Corporate Democracies

What, then, distinguishes the Western, liberal conception of democracy from the corporatist versions found elsewhere? It is perhaps not too unfair to suggest that this lies in the extent to which, in the liberal view of things, citizens are supposed to have a free and unfettered say in where their own good and that of the community lie. Elsewhere, by contrast, certain broad directions of policy are regarded as given (Macpherson, 1966, pp. 33–4) and rival parties and ideologies are ruled out.

It is important not to exaggerate this difference, or to fall into the trap of naïvely representing Eastern bloc governments merely as bigoted and tyrannical men and women determined to impose their own conception of things. Communist governments and other communist organisations set considerable store by collective leadership, constitutionality, self-criticism and such things as the structure of committees and representation (Margolis, 1979, p. 27). For their part, liberal democratic governments expect and may even compel a considerable degree of loyalty and self-censorship from their subjects on important matters in times of crisis.

Despite these reservations, however, there remains within the general notion of a democracy an important difference between a state in which the government formally recognises the right of opposition, criticism and other means by which it may be made sensitive to what people actually want and one in which, for whatever reason, the government takes it upon itself to determine what the people's good is, or within what limits it may be found.

These contrary views of democracy reflect differing understandings of the relationship between the individual and the community to which he belongs, and two different conceptions of the function of government. Both views have their antecedents in the political writings of the seventeenth and eighteenth centuries. Common to many of these was the myth of a 'state of nature' following which men were brought together and united by some form of social contract or contracts.

Just what were supposed to be the conditions under which men lived in a state of nature, and more especially the form of the contracts men were supposed to have made with each other, are all-important. According to one version of the theory, men in a state of nature lived, if not in a state of war, then at least under primitive if, perhaps, idyllic conditions. On this theory all the benefits and advantages of an organised existence are owed to the contract and to the community or state it created. For convenience I refer to this as the Rousseauist view, though some people may regard this as a libel on Rousseau, whose views are anything but consistent and easy to summarise.

On this view the 'sovereignty of the people' is absolute and undivided. The citizen who owes all to the community has no grounds for opposing the community's will. Opposition may be treasonable, and may be combated by all means within the government's power. Implicit in this view is the distinction which is to be drawn between, on the one hand, the 'will of the people' or 'general will', and on the other, what individual people actually want. As individuals, people may be misled by 'lying propaganda'. From this they may need to be protected not only by the control of information, but also by a strenuous and uncompromising dose of 'political education' in youth and adolescence.

By contrast, according to what it is proposed to label a Lockean view, man is an independent, rational and moral being with purposes of his own even prior to the social state, and simply unites with others for the greater security of his rights and purposes. Consequently, the essential feature of this view, which underlies much Western political theory, is that individuals do not owe their independence, way of life, or most important rights to the state, and are therefore perfectly entitled to resist the incursions of the state if their independence, way of life, or fundamental rights are threatened by it.

Since individuals have rationality and purposes independently of their membership of the state on this view, they may differ among themselves about these purposes, and will often be in conflict. There being no infallible way of judging between the value of different people's purposes and insights, toleration is called for. The function of government is limited to protecting pre-existing rights. Individuals may have rights against governments, including governments supported by majorities. Above all, there is no warrant for limiting information or for preventing minorities from attempting to transform themselves into majorities by persuading others to join them. Nor, on this view, is there any justification for suppressing independent organisations or other centres of activity and values, or attempting to bend them to the purposes of the state as a whole.

It must be conceded, however, that this view of liberal democracy in which government exists simply to carry out whatever requirements the 'people' chooses to place upon it raises a number of difficulties. These are of both a philosophical and an empirical kind.

## Theoretical Difficulties in the Classical Theory of Liberal Democracy

If, like Rousseau, we see the 'people' or the state as an entity transcending the individuals that compose it, then it may be plausible to represent the people as having purposes, a destiny, or even a 'will' of its own. This 'will' may not be consciously shared by all the individuals that compose it, or even by a very substantial number of them, though it may in principle be 'detected' and followed by those who see themselves as appointed or authorised to govern. But if as in the Western version of democratic theory no such entity is posited, it is much harder, especially in the modern world, to understand what would be meant by the claim that government is being carried on according to the people's will.

The model of democracy implied by liberal democratic theory in what is often called its classical form is that of the small community, the Greek city-state, Swiss canton, or Quaker meeting. Such a community would be composed of persons of similar interests, knowledge and outlook jointly managing affairs which are comprehensible to all. These might include the regulation of trade, mutual security, the upkeep of public places, public works, and so on. For convenience as the community grows larger, so the theory goes, it might appoint experts or representatives to carry out its business for it, but in the end what is done will be understood and approved by most of the people in the community. Decisions taken by representatives are still supposed to be in accordance with the community's wishes in a way that is often compared to the 'sense of the meeting' in the Quaker meeting-house. The people are supposed to remain sovereign, in fact as well as in name.

As society becomes more complex the good citizen is, on this theory, supposed to keep himself informed about all matters relating to community affairs, take part in local and national election campaigns, lobby his representatives on matters of importance and ensure that representatives are well briefed on the wishes of himself and other citizens. Only on this condition can the representatives be expected to do the job of representing their constituents properly.

Quite clearly, however, there may in the modern state often exist no common view of what is to be done that is shared and understood by all members of the community. Recourse may be had to the device of majority voting as an expedient. But saying that the will of the people means the will of the majority of the people raises almost as many problems as it solves. It is far from clear that the majority of people have any specific will on many of the issues government is called upon to decide. Nor is it universally accepted that democratic representatives can be regarded as bound or mandated by the detailed wishes of those who elect them. In any case, if the will of the people simply means the wishes of the majority of individuals who compose it, it is hard to see why those who are not members of the majority should feel bound to subordinate their own wishes to those of the majority.

It may seem possible to solve some of these problems by saying that in a democracy the voter is expected to vote, not for policies he thinks will be in his own personal interest, but for those he thinks will be in the general or public interest. But there is no certainty, indeed not much likelihood, that this will happen. More important from a philosophical point of view, pinning down just precisely what is the public interest is not a straightforward matter (P. White, 1971).

It may often be the case that no common or general interest can be identified. In the modern state based on differentiated roles and the division of labour, measures which favour one group may often be detrimental to the interests of others. Measures relating to taxation, social benefits and industrial relations are cases in point. Individuals may also have radically different and incompatible evaluations of what constitutes the public good. Building an opera house at public expense or granting permission to open a night club in a small town would raise issues of this kind.

So much for the theoretical problems involved in the notion of a liberal democratic government ruling in accordance with the wishes of the electorate. In recent years, however, social scientists investigating the political understanding and behaviour of voters have produced what appear to be even more devastating criticisms of the classical theory of liberal democracy in which governments are supposed to rule in accordance with the wishes of an intelligent, critical and well-informed citizenry.

## Empirical Problems for the Classical Theory of Liberal Democracy

The first and most obvious empirical argument against the notion of democracy as government in accordance with the wishes of the population as a whole is the great complexity of government decisions in the modern world. We attach little value to the layman's opinion in the fields of nuclear physics and brain surgery, so why should we rely on it in matters of economics and government? It may be countered that a businessman who knows little of electronics or law may entrust such matters to experts to sort out for him. So may not electors likewise choose the general ends of policy they wish to see achieved, and entrust the complex and technical task of bringing them about to their appointed representatives?

Unfortunately, the analogy is misleading. Politicians do not usually employ technical expertise to bring about ends specifically chosen by the electorate. As often as not the important choices they have to make on behalf of the electorate concern ends rather than means. A left-wing politician may, in mid-term, have to choose between his own and his supporters' inclinations towards pacifism and a policy of taking up arms against a fascist aggressor. Similarly, a conservative may have to choose between relatively free-trade policies and the protection of local interests in his constituency.

Nor is it possible to argue that politicians simply choose between the best means of achieving 'social justice' or 'prosperity'. One employs the professional expert for much more specific ends than these. When, furthermore, an expert such as a doctor, lawyer, engineer, or whatever, is employed by a private individual he is expected to explain to his principal the risks and disadvantages of the steps he proposes to undertake on his client's behalf.

Politicians, by contrast, do not dispassionately set forth the various good and bad effects of their policies so that electors can make an informed and rational choice between them. Socialist politicians tend to under-estimate the tax cost of the social reforms they advocate and right-wing politicians have little to say at election time about the social miseries that are likely to be caused by 'reducing public spending'. For a lawyer or engineer to fail to draw his client's attention to the likely disadvantages of the steps he is about to take on his behalf would be unconscionable.

No actual choice of individual policies is placed before the electorate. At election time one votes not for individual policies but for party packages. Many people may, for example, favour Labour policy on industrial relations and education, but regard Labour defence policy as suicidal. Consequently, even a party that gains a clear majority of votes at a general election cannot say of all the policies included in its manifesto, 'These are the express wishes of those whom we are obliged to serve'.

In any case, governments in Western democracies are rarely supported by a majority of those eligible to vote and are by no means always supported by a majority of those who actually do so. This problem would only partly be solved by electoral reform and systems of proportional representation. In that case it is likely that governments would be formed by coalitions between parties whose supporters might be bitterly opposed to each other on some matters. The results of elections would still turn on the abstentions of the disillusioned as much as on the positive choices of those who supported the parties of government.

It cannot be said that the political parties and their leaders reflect the opinions and prevailing ideologies of the electorate. On the contrary, their role is rather to form, propagate and win support for those ideologies.

The vulnerability of the electorate to single issues of immediate emotional appeal is well known. Lloyd George's infamous 'Hang the Kaiser' campaign, the American vote for Prohibition and various 'red scares' are frequently quoted in support of this point. Politicians pay great attention to the presence of their photograph and selected information about their personal and family lives on their election literature, and are particularly sensitive to 'smears' regarding their activities unconnected with politics. Yet none of these things would be of much importance if the electorate could be relied on to cast its vote on the strength of policies alone.

Empirical research (Berelson, Lazarsfeld and McPhee, 1954; Almond and Verba, 1965; see also Margolis, 1979, pp. 96–125) has revealed that the electorate is far from being the body of interested, involved, enlightened democrats the 'classical theory' of liberal democracy requires it to be. Numerous studies have found that only about a third of adult populations in Britain and America even claim to follow politics regularly and a similar proportion profess little or no interest even at election times.

Surveys have also shown that though most members of the public claim to have opinions on important political matters, few of those with opinions take any steps whatever to propagate their views or have them implemented. Though pollsters are successful in eliciting political opinions from members of the public, voters are surprisingly ignorant regarding the working of the political system, the level of government responsible for various public institutions and services and, above all, the actual policies of the major parties on many issues.

By contrast, some members of the public are found to be extremely knowledgeable about issues that directly concern them. Though defenders of the classical theory may be tempted to find some small crumb of comfort in this fact, it must be pointed out that a high degree of knowledge and involvement in limited, specific areas is scarcely likely to make for balanced judgement in the consideration of national and international policies as a whole.

## An Alternative Theory of Democracy

In view of the above, some political theorists (Schumpeter, 1954, pp. 250–302; Dahl, 1956) have argued that the essence of liberal democracy lies not in popular choice between policies at all, but in the competition between various elites for the right to govern. Elections, that is, simply provide the arena in which various elites compete for the votes of the electorate. In contrast to the classical theory, such a view is claimed to have the advantage of not resting on assumptions about the involvement and competences of the average voter which are manifestly false.

Adherents of this 'alternative theory' are able to claim a number of further advantages. Unlike the classical theory, for example, this theory is able to account for the phenomena of political leadership and the initiation of policies. On this latter point the classical theory is notoriously unsatisfactory, since complex pieces of legislation clearly do not simply emerge from the populace like the sense of a Quaker meeting.

It may also be held with some plausibility that on this view government remains sensitive to people's felt needs, wishes and views, however well or ill informed these may be. On the assumption that in casting their vote electors have some regard to the government's record, the government is motivated to avoid obvious tyranny and incompetence. Electors may be relatively fair-minded on matters that do not directly affect their own interests, so that governments are normally well advised not to be seen to act too unjustly even towards small and powerless minorities and individuals. The one exception to this is where a conspicuous minority can be transformed into a target for hostility and prejudice.

In political debate both constructive presentation of supposed alternative policies *and* criticism of the government's performance become legitimate. On the classical theory one would expect somewhat more specific alternative policies than are normally forthcoming from parliamentary oppositions. Also, that theory tends to regard 'negative' criticism of the government's performance as rather unworthy. On the alternative theory the opposition essentially represents not a gamut of alternative policies but simply an alternative government so that, in the true spirit of the market economy, if the electorate does not like the service it is getting it may take its custom elsewhere.

If parties tend to hug the middle of the political road that is perfectly all right, not only because centrist policies are those that appeal to most people and are less intensely disliked, but because as far as the electorate is concerned choosing between different policies is not the main object of the exercise anyway.

The alternative theory also confers respectability on the activities of lobbies and pressure groups which play such an important part in politics in the West. On the classical theory these were regarded as somewhat disreputable since they represented sectional interests rather than the public interest as a whole. But in some versions of the alternative theory which speak enthusiastically about 'polyarchy' or 'pluralism' (Dahl, 1956) interest groups and their competing efforts to influence the government of the day are seen as the very essence of liberal democratic politics.

If ordinary members of the public have not the time, ability, energy, or inclination to inform themselves or become involved in politics, the leaders and officials of their interest groups – environmental lobbies, trade and professional associations, trade unions, and so on – will do it for them. All the ordinary member of the public has to do is to join or associate himself with his particular interest group to enable his spokesman to put his case on behalf of such-and-such a number of voters.

Despite its explanatory value, however, the 'alternative theory' has not gone uncriticised, and has a number of unattractive features. It is, for example, difficult to know just what to make of the notion of electors choosing a government without some reference to the policies they expect it to try to implement. Critics have also contested the theory's claim to be purely descriptive rather than normative (Lively, 1975, pp. 76–88; Margolis, 1979, pp. 113–23). Parts of many works adopting an 'alternative theory' point of view read rather like conscious or unconscious apologies for the status quo in Western, especially Anglo-Saxon, countries. The ethical implications of the alternative theory for liberal democracies will be discussed in greater detail in Chapter 3. For the moment it suffices to say that the theory has the effect of pre-empting the ideologically valuable label 'democracy' for a set-up which, if it is as the theory describes it, is morally dubious and elitist in the emphasis it places on the distinction between government and the governed.

## Participatory Democracy

Most of what has been said so far applies to democracy and democratic government at the level of the nation or state, both in the West and elsewhere. The arguments I have considered relate to such institutions as Parliament, Congress and other national assemblies. Depending on which theory of liberal democracy one holds one might expect the citizen in the West either to vote in a naïve, uninformed manner, or to take a keen interest in politics, inform himself on the key issues, discuss them with others before voting, and so on. Either way the citizen's role

15

is limited to voting or at most lobbying his representative and perhaps attempting to influence him by the assurance of electoral support or implied threat of support for an opponent. On both theories the, in Britain, quinquennial act of voting is the consummation and climax of the ordinary citizen's political interest and activity.

To see democracy as applicable only to the institutions of national or even local authority government, however, is to fail to take account of the importance in our everyday lives of a great deal of discussion, collective decision-making and even occasionally formal voting. These procedures may be used not only in the institutional apparatus of government but also in much more homely institutions such as sports and social clubs, voluntary associations and societies and even families and informal groups deciding what to do or how to arrange their affairs. Such groupings may operate either more or less democratically, but many of them employ some degree of democracy some of the time.

To see democracy as applicable only to the formal apparatus of government is also to accept that many of the things that affect us in important ways will not be subject to democratic control at all, or if they are then only in a very indirect and distant kind of way. The institutions in which most of us spend the greater part of our lives – commercial firms, the armed services, educational institutions – are often not the least bit democratic, but are hierarchical, not to say authoritarian.

Since the beginning of the 1970s it has become fashionable for writers to speak of participatory or more tendentiously 'new' democratic theory (Megill, 1970; Pateman, 1970) urging a greater degree of democratic participation at all levels in institutions, political parties, industry and the community. Some groups have been interested in establishing community or 'street' committees on 'soulless' housing estates, others in motorway and other environmental protest groups. The short-lived push for greater pupil and student participation in the government of schools and universities and attempts to encourage various forms of industrial or 'workplace' democracy (P. White, 1979) may also be seen as part of this movement.

The defining feature of 'participatory' democracy is not the formal sovereignty of the people whose will must somehow be obeyed. Nor, certainly, does it lie in a simple choice by members, workers, residents, or whatever, between representative members of various elites who will make decisions or take action for them. On the contrary, the point of participatory democracy is that those involved, those who will be most affected by the decision to be made or the action to be taken, actually take part in the discussion and take the decision, and the responsibility for the decision, themselves.

Even where, for one reason or another, responsibility for decisions has to be borne by persons other than those most immediately affected, the notion of participatory democracy implies that those to be substantially affected by the decision shall at least be seriously consulted, and the reasons for the decision explained and defended publicly. It is also part of the thinking behind the movement for greater participation that if formal democracy in governments is ineffectual in changing the conditions of our lives, then we should set about collectively controlling those things that most immediately impinge upon our existence. And we should do it ourselves, rather than leave it to others who may be less immediately committed to our point of view.

In many of the situations in which participatory democracy is urged, in community and voluntary associations, in academic institutions and above all in the workplace, those most affected by whatever decisions are taken will be precisely those who have to carry out these decisions. Participatory democracy at this level, therefore, is not vulnerable to the criticism which has been levelled at the classical theory of liberal democracy, namely, that it involves ordinary individuals in irresponsibly opting for policies in which they have otherwise shown little interest, and whose merits they are incompetent to judge. On the contrary, those involved in the exercise of participatory democracy will frequently be those most qualified by direct experience to decide on the matter in hand, and those with the strongest motives for deciding responsibly and judiciously.

It was noted above that the theory of participatory democracy is sometimes tendentiously referred to as the 'new' democratic theory. This is something of a misnomer. The notion of democracy as direct participation and discussion by those involved in decisions to be taken is at least as old as the word itself. For, as we saw earlier, it is upon just such a model of democracy in small communities such as Greek city-states, and so on, that the classical theory of liberal democracy is based, and to which modern representative democracy forms at best a very imperfect approximation.

## Democracy as a Way of Life or Set of Values

Brief reference must finally be made to one use of the word democracy and its adjective democratic to describe a community or milieu without being primarily concerned with its political institutions, or with the actual distribution of power it embodies. Child-centred educators, for example, may use the term to refer to a non-authoritarian style of education in which learning takes place, not as a result of the authoritative say-so of the teacher, but as a result of the pupil's own efforts and experience.

Other writers may employ the term to mean simply 'informal' (Benn and Peters, 1959, p. 333). To say that in this sense a school or firm has become 'more democratic' may not imply that there has been any modification of the power structure, but merely that members of different levels of the hierarchy now address each other by their christian names, that 'within reason' those at lower levels are permitted or even encouraged to speak their minds, and that formal reminders of rank and status are minimised.

Writers may also speak of democratic societies as those in which certain so-called 'democratic values' prevail, notably those of freedom, equality and consideration of interests (P. White, 1971, p. 21).

## Conclusion

In this chapter certain contrasting views of democracy have been considered. Despite deep differences between these, it has been suggested that democracies have at least one thing in common: that in some sense of the term the good of the people is supposed to be the prime purpose for which the state and other institutions exist. Distinctions have been drawn between the liberal democracies of the West and the corporate or 'people's' democracies existing elsewhere. Two views of the former (the so-called classical and alternative theories) have been explored. A contrast has been drawn between representative and participatory democracy. Reference has also been made to use of the term democracy to refer not to the institutions of government but to a style of life or set of values.

# 3

# *Justifying Democracy*

Arguments in favour of liberal democracy are mainly of two kinds. First, there are what may be termed arguments from efficiency. These are arguments to the effect that a country or institution that is governed democratically will be governed better than one that is not. Secondly, there are arguments from individual rights – that is, arguments to the effect that, better governed or not, people have a right to be governed, or govern themselves, democratically rather than in any other way.

## Arguments from Efficiency

It may seem surprising that anyone should think liberal democracy a particularly efficient form of government. Surely it must at least be more efficient for one person, or a small group of people, to give orders which are obeyed without argument, rather than go in for the endless debating that seems to characterise democratic institutions. 'All talk and no action' is a criticism frequently made of democracy, and even its defenders are sometimes inclined to admit that democracy is inefficient, while claiming that its inefficiency is outweighed by other virtues. In particular it is often urged against liberal democracy that it is inclined to subject the views of the few to those of the many, hence of the intelligent to the mediocre.

Yet if democracy is so inefficient a form of polity it is hard to understand why, in recent years, the number of democratic states of various kinds has fairly steadily increased at the expense of other regimes, while remaining explicitly non-democratic regimes around the world are increasingly under pressure, and are not expected to survive indefinitely. Even wars between dictatorships and democracies do not invariably end in victory for the former, yet war would seem to be an activity in which sheer efficiency and centralisation was an advantage.

19

Indeed, some supporters of democracy are inclined to point to the example of the Second World War as evidence that, in the long run, democracy is not only morally preferable to dictatorship but also the more expedient way for a state to organise itself. The achievements of dictators, it is sometimes suggested, are limited to spectacular early gains, and such mechanical matters as getting trains to run on time. Despite their centralised power, dictatorships are notoriously unstable, and dictators and tyrants are commonly depicted as going in constant fear of their own subjects.

Despite apparent inefficiencies, a number of reasons may be put forward as to why democracy may be expected to prove a more effective form of government than most. The first of these is the so-called feedback argument which owes much to Popper (1961, pp. 58–118) and is in essence as follows. The world is a complex place, and human knowledge is not innate. We can only learn about the world and how to cope with it by intelligent trial and error, by hypothesis and refutation. Feedback about how we are getting on is essential if we are to succeed in any practical undertaking in the world. This is particularly true in the social and political world where conditions and the opinions and reactions of individuals are constantly changing.

Given the complexity of the world, democratic governments would seem to have the great advantage of being able to utilise the combined knowledge and judgement of all citizens, or of as many as are actively involved in the political process. Criticism and the presentation of reasons and evidence in favour of alternative policies are an essential part of liberal democracy at least, and denial of the right of criticism is widely regarded as undemocratic. To the dictator, the subject who argues for alternative policies is an insubordinate, a threat. But by suppressing him the dictator not only deprives himself of the dissenter's knowledge and judgement, but also discourages others from offering opinions or reporting information which may be uncongenial to the ruler. But if one is to rule successfully, or indeed do anything properly in a world of which one's knowledge is necessarily incomplete, one is more likely to be efficient when surrounded by honest critics than by flatterers.

Liberal democracy not only allows and encourages dissatisfied citizens to express their dissatisfaction; it also provides motivation for the rivals of the current government to take up, and no doubt magnify, the complaints of the discontented. It further ensures that government will be sensitive to the complaints of those upon whose votes it will depend at the next election. Besides improving the efficiency of government by making it sensitive to the reactions of the governed, liberal democracy also enables larger changes of policy direction, and changes of rulers, to take place smoothly without violence or upheaval.

A second reason why democracies are supposed to run more efficiently than non-democratic regimes is that people feel more committed to decisions which they have a hand in making than to carrying out orders handed down from above. One is, after all, in some sense committed to an arrangement one has given one's support to, and may feel some responsibility for making it work. This might seem to be an advantage possessed only by small, participatory democracies rather than by the modern state. Nevertheless, even in representative democracies it is sometimes argued, though not it must be admitted entirely convincingly, that a ground of political obligation in the democratic state resides in the fact that the citizen who disagrees with the law may attempt to change it by democratic means. Where the possibility of democratic change exists, the argument goes – and some people may be convinced by it – insurrection is unjustified.

Thirdly, it may be argued that the democratic process is likely to throw up good leaders. This may seem surprising as the professional politician is often caricatured as a shifty compromiser, or even an out-and-out rogue. This, however, is only a popular image and it has not been shown that men and women in public life are actually less worthy of esteem than anyone else. Indeed, politicians of all shades of opinion do appear to share a capacity to devote themselves tirelessly to their profession and to the service of the public as they see it. That the motive of service may be mixed with vainglory and personal ambition does not necessarily mean that they perform their task less well. Given the complexities of the modern world, politicians capable of compromise may be more suitable to govern than men and women of unbending principle. And given even limited freedom of the press and the motives which both professional journalists and rival politicians have for revealing the misdeeds of those in power, there is reason to hope that out-and-out scoundrels will eventually be revealed for what they are.

Fourthly, it has been argued (Nelson, 1980, pp. 94–129) that a liberal democratic government is likely to rule justly. This is because, as we have seen, criticism of both policies and leaders is integral to the liberal democratic process. Opponents of the government have a vested interest in drawing attention to injustices and abuses and these, if too blatant, may alienate even those not directly affected by them.

## The Argument from Equality of Rights

The arguments in favour of democracy considered so far rest on the assumption that certain effects will result from the practice of democracy which are not likely to be produced under other forms of government. In contrast to these, the argument now to be considered has the great advantage that it does not depend on supposed and, it must be admitted, somewhat speculative claims about the effects of democracy. It does not, indeed, depend on anything so contingent as outcomes or effects at all.

The argument from equality of rights requires some explanation for it is frequently misunderstood and often rejected on the basis of such an inadequate understanding. In its valid and defensible form the argument is not that people are equal in rights because they share some other common feature such as membership of a particular species, or the possession of some quality or achievement like rationality or the use of language.

It is not clear why membership of a certain species or the possession of certain capacities should in themselves confer rights. Certain skills and attributes may be necessary conditions for participating in government, as they are for any other distinctively human activity, but it is not obvious that they entitle anyone to do so. The claim that people are equal in rights does not depend on the presence of any unifying characteristic at all. It depends rather on the absence of any convincing reason why any person should consider himself the natural subordinate of, or less important than, any other. (For the classic statement of this argument, see Locke [1690], Second Treatise, ch. 2, para. 6.)

Many societies, not excluding the Greeks, have, of course, persisted in regarding some individuals as the natural inferiors or subordinates of others. In some societies one may be expected even as an adult to obey one's elder brother or one's father, or the members of a particular family, race, or sex. Both subordinates and superiors may be socialised into believing that this is the proper and natural order of things.

But there is no reason why those cast in subordinate roles should concur in such inequitable arrangements if they do not see it as being in their interest to do so. We may find it useful and prudent to follow the advice and allow ourselves to be ruled by those who are older, cleverer, or more experienced than ourselves. At a pinch some people might even look for guidance to those who, by virtue of family background and social position, are more accustomed to directing the community's affairs. But that does not constitute an obligation to obey if we do not choose to do so.

This does not mean that individuals are morally free to do just as they like. We may, for example, feel that we have an obligation to obey the rules of our society in return for the many benefits we enjoy as a result of the fact that these rules are obeyed by others – provided the rules are not too arbitrary and the benefits not too sparse or uncertain. We ought, perhaps, not to hurt people who do not hurt us, or take or damage their belongings, or prevent them doing what they want to do provided they are not harming or interfering with others.

But these obligations do not arise from any further obligation to obey some superior authority. On the contrary, they may be shown to be the consequence of just that equality that is here under discussion. If all are independent and mutually non-subordinate in the way suggested, no one is warranted in interfering with others without good grounds. Those who have not yet achieved rationality, or have temporarily or permanently lost any rationality they may have had, ought no doubt to be looked after and controlled in some aspects of their lives by others. But the great majority of mankind do not fall into this category once they have grown up.

Now if people are not naturally subordinate to one another, there is no reason why anyone should accept any arrangement for co-ordinating our collective affairs, that is, any system of government, that accords him less right to consideration or a less than equal degree of influence than others over what is to be done. It may also be thought a consequence of the principle of equal consideration that individuals may reasonably expect to have a particular say in matters that especially affect their interests or concern them closely.

It would be absurd to suggest that anything approaching such equality of influence and consideration in arranging a community's affairs exists in any modern state, or has ever existed in any group of any size. Ultimately, however, something of this kind must be seen as the ideal of democracy, and states and institutions in the real world may be regarded as more or less democratic as they approach or recede from this ideal.

Many of the procedures which we regard as part and parcel of modern democracy – representation, majority voting, free speech, entrenched basic rights – may be evaluated in terms of whether or not they are the best possible procedures for bringing such an ideal about. We may also use this ideal as a yardstick against which to assess the various conceptions of democracy that were considered in Chapter 2.

## Equal Influence and Consideration and Corporate Democracies

It is not altogether clear that the ideal I have proposed commits us to the Western, liberal brand of democracy, as opposed to other kinds of democracy existing elsewhere. One-party democracies may seem to be disqualified by the fact that some policy options are ruled out in a rather doctrinaire way, and opportunities for power are in reality only open to party members. Against this, however, it may be held that intra-party systems of committees and representation are such as to afford adequate consideration to everyone's views and interests. More convincingly, perhaps, especially in the developing world, it may be argued that the present system leads to policies which most people would approve of if they were adequately informed and fully conscious of the true situation. Though the present regime does give undue power to the 'vanguard' or elite of party officials, this may be the best approach to the ideal that can be achieved at this particular stage of the people's historical development, while any other arrangement would lead to less rather than more equality of consideration and influence.

Marxist writers in particular always insist on the transient nature of present inequalities of power. Readers will doubtless have their own views of the validity of such a position, which is undoubtedly held with great sincerity in many parts of the world. It must also be admitted that whether Western liberal democracy can possibly be justified by reference to the ideal suggested above must also depend in part on the answers to certain questions. In particular, it would seem to depend on whether some approach to democracy as depicted by the classical theory or that invoked by adherents of participatory democracy is possible, or whether ultimately liberal democracies are always bound to approximate to the state of affairs described by the alternative theory, in which most citizens do not have a hand in choosing policies but are limited to a narrow choice between the elites who are to govern for them.

This being so, we must return briefly to re-examine the classical and alternative theories of liberal democracy and the notion of participatory democracy outlined in Chapter 2. In so doing we shall pay particular attention to the question of justification in the light of the ideal of equal influence and equal consideration. It is convenient to begin with the alternative theory whose validity as an explanatory theory must to some extent come into question, as well as the ethical acceptability of the situation it purports to describe.

## Equal Influence and Consideration and the Alternative Theory

If equality of influence is to be the test, it is difficult to regard liberal democracies as described by the alternative theory as democracies at all. According to that theory in its extreme form, citizens do not themselves exercise any influence over what is done. They are not supposed to choose between policies, and certainly do not originate policies, but simply choose between rulers who will govern as they, the chosen rulers, think appropriate.

It must, of course, be admitted that even this constitutes a small advance on regimes in which people have to accept the rule of the individual who happens to be born into a certain family at a certain time, are given a ruler by a colonising power, or fall subject to the power of a dictator or military junta as the result of a coup. Also, if the electorate chooses its government, even from a very limited range of possible candidates, it presumably has reasons of a kind for choosing this government rather than that. It must at least be presumed that electors vote for the government they expect to govern in the kind of way they prefer. If this were not so, we could not speak of the electorate as 'choosing a government' at all.

To this extent, therefore, the claim that the electorate chooses between alternative governments and not between policies must be seen as an exaggeration. New policies may be initiated after an election. Party manifestos may play down genuinely problematical issues. Electors may be faced with choices between limited numbers of party packages, none of which may be entirely to their liking. Elections may sometimes be won and lost on single, relatively unimportant, emotional issues, or on the basis of some trivial matter such as the party leader's charisma or personal appearance, or public performance on a particular occasion.

All of these things may be conceded, but it remains true that at least one important way in which potential governments compete for votes is by means of the policies they offer, and by criticising those of their rivals. If the range of policies offered is limited, this may be partly because no others are likely to command wide support. Though many voters may feel unhappy about some parts of their party's electoral package, these packages are not put together in an entirely arbitrary way. They necessarily have a certain coherence and reflect underlying views about how certain priorities and the interests of certain groups are to be ordered.

Manifestos may be only loosely adhered to, but it is difficult and unwise for a party to disregard too obviously what it has said it will try to do, for that would be to offer too vulnerable a flank to its opponents. Emotional and personal issues may tip the balance in a closely fought election, but are unlikely to persuade the electorate to accept policies which are blatantly incompetent or evil. Finally, though parties to some degree form rather than follow public opinion, they cannot get the public to swallow just any policy but must have some regard to the sort of measures electors are likely to see as desirable.

So even someone committed to the ideal of democracy as a society in which all are equally considered and equally able to influence matters of common concern may see the situation described by the alternative theory as the beginnings of an approach to that ideal. What must be rejected, however, is any suggestion that the alternative theory provides a justification for attempting to preserve the present state of affairs rather than working for conditions under which the ideal may be more fully realised.

Despite the alternative theory's claims to objectivity, writers adopting this point of view often describe the status quo in Western countries with complacency or approval. In particular some such writers are inclined to welcome the situation in which the great majority of the population take little significant part in the political process on the grounds that it is favourable or even essential to stability (Lively, 1975, p. 79).

On this view, an appropriate political and civic education for the majority would discourage activism and stress the importance of accepting the 'democratic authority' of elected leaders. Alternative theorists are highly sceptical of the desirability of any great degree of popular participation which 'overloads' the system and may lead to destabilisation. For them it is important that citizens should respect established institutions and the existing rules of the game. These enable the personnel of government to be changed without upheaval, and preserve the illusion that the common man can get things changed through the ballot box.

But though in general stability is preferable to anarchy, stability in itself is a necessary rather than a sufficient condition of a satisfactory polity. Despotic regimes may be extremely stable. The alternative theory describes and by implication often gives support to a situation which is essentially elitist, distinguishing sharply between 'them' and 'us', between government and the governed. Those who are not members of the government or potential governing elites, or possibly the leaders of pressure groups, are condemned to the passive role of making infrequent and highly limited choices at elections or occasional referendums.

Where such a distinction between government and the governed is emphasised and represented as desirable there can be little pretence of taking equality of influence and consideration as one's aim. Such a situation gives ruling elites considerable scope to place their own group interests before those of the community, particularly if the members of rival elites are drawn from or aspire to a particular social class. If government is from the outset limited to relatively small groups, some interests will always have more favourable opportunities for access to and influence on members of the government than others.

If, therefore, it is thought that the alternative theory describes something approaching reality in Western states their defender must, rather like the Marxist, concede that the regime under which he lives is far from ideal and look to possibilities of change that will enable the aim of equality of influence and consideration to be approached more nearly.

# Equality of Influence and Consideration and the Classical Theory

Unlike the alternative theory, the much-maligned classical theory of democracy does not usually pretend to be descriptive. Many of its early proponents were arguing for change at a time when not only were governments not democratic, but most people did not even think that democracy was desirable in principle. Given, however, that the current situation is still far from satisfactory to the committed democrat, it is relevant to ask whether some version of the classical theory remains an adequate basis for the advocation of the further changes that are required today.

Justification of democracy in terms of moral independence and equal rights to consideration and influence would seem a reasonable interpretation of the ideals of liberty and equality upon which the early supporters of democracy based their case. To a large extent problems connected with the 'will of the people' disappear if we think in terms not of the right of 'the people' collectively to be obeyed, but of the equal right of individuals to influence collective decisions.

This does not mean that individuals have actually to exert equal influence on all collective decisions. Not all citizens will be equally concerned to influence all decisions. A particular citizen may be keen to exert influence on some matters but not much bothered about others. What is required is that the system should not hinder or prevent some individuals from exerting influence on government while making it relatively easy for others to do so. It is also necessary that the vast majority of individuals should not be misled by an ideology to the effect that it is inappropriate or impossible for them to try to change things, or wilfully left in a state of ignorance about how to do it.

As regards the classical theorists' supposedly over-optimistic view of the average citizen's capabilities, it is not clear that ordinary people are as incompetent to judge the broad lines of party policies as the empirical findings of alternative theorists claim to show. What various surveys actually show is that many electors are ignorant or hesitant about certain rather detailed matters of fact – the names of ministers, the division of powers between local and central government, details of policies – all of which may seem ludicrously elementary to those familiar with them. The policy issues that divide the parties, at least in present-day Britain, are not matters of factual detail, but broad questions of value.

With some simplification the issue may be seen as one between the just claims of good fortune, effort and initiative on the one hand and those of security and need on the other. The moderately affluent voter is faced with a fairly clear choice of whether he himself would rather have more money in his pocket, or whether he would rather see various

27

public services such as health, education and various forms of welfare provision more adequately funded. This is not a question of detailed knowledge, or even of ratiocination. Collectively we may sometimes get the balance between the above alternatives wrong. This is both our right and our responsibility. We do not need to nominate rulers to make that kind of decision for us. Nor, in choosing between candidates who have already identified themselves with policies of the left or right, do we do so.

If, as members of the public, we need more political sophistication it is to enable us to distinguish political rhetoric from relevant fact and argument, so that we can discern how faithfully those we have elected have striven to implement the priorities for which we as electors have opted. It may be thought that the political knowledge and understanding of most electors currently falls short of such requirements. This, however, does not show that ordinary citizens should restrict themselves to judging the general character and competence of political candidates and leave matters of policy to those that know better. On the contrary, it suggests that a government committed to democracy should have as one of its priorities the provision of a programme of political education which would enable the generality of electors to acquire a degree of political understanding approaching that supposedly possessed by the small number of citizens who were politically enfranchised in previous centuries.

If the classical theory has a fairly serious shortcoming as a theory of advocation, it is that in concerning itself primarily with central government, as noted earlier, it neglects important areas of people's lives which impinge on them more directly than the actions of government. Even this criticism, however, should not be exaggerated. Though it may be important to democratise the actual institutions in which people spend their everyday lives, the importance to us of the overall framework of government is very great.

Centrally determined policies govern the balance of power between such groups as management and workers, police and protesters, consumers and producers. Though such policies may not seem to affect our lives so immediately as decisions taken at our place of work or in our own neighbourhood, their effect is pervasive. Decisions at central government level may do much to encourage or hinder the development of democratic procedures and attitudes at more local levels.

## Equality of Influence and Consideration and Participatory Democracy

If the underlying justification of democracy is the right of all to equal influence and consideration in matters that affect us collectively, and correspondingly more say in those that affect us most closely, this ideal would seem to be best realised in a society in which as many opportunities as possible exist for democratic participation at all levels including those that affect the individual most closely in his daily life.

Opponents of participatory democracy are quick to caricature this suggestion and to bring out the absurdities it might seem to imply. Attention may be drawn to the apparent contradiction involved in forcing people to take part in decision-making when they would much rather leave such matters to others (Wilson and Cowell, 1983, p. 112). Democratic decision-making procedures, it is sometimes said, are notoriously cumbersome and ardent democrats are often depicted as spending hours discussing trivia. The stock of anti-participatory rhetoric also includes reference to employers being told by employees how to run 'their own' businesses, hospital porters debating on equal terms with brain-surgeons over how to perform a delicate operation, and captains of warships being obliged to call meetings before activating their vessels' defences against an approaching missile.

We might well dismiss such gibes out of hand on the grounds that only someone determined to discredit democracy would attempt to put it into operation in such a literal-minded way. Some of them do, however, arise from quite proper queries about participatory democracy which it is appropriate to deal with here.

First of all, the right to exert equal influence in any matter does not entail the duty to do so. The moral agent cannot abdicate responsibility for what is done in his name, but it is perfectly consistent with the notion of participatory democracy for people, both individually and collectively, to agree to allow some decisions to be made by others, and to abide by those decisions. Rights may, after all, be waived. All that is required is that the possibility of taking part in the making of decisions should be preserved. This, however, entails more than formal or constitutional opportunities. The opportunities must be genuine in the sense that people must know about them and be aware of their value as a means of controlling and safeguarding or improving the conditions of their own lives.

There is no reason why democrats should not delegate some decisions, especially trivial ones. Nor is there any reason in principle why democratic meetings should be more inefficient than others. No businessman would miss a board meeting at which matters affecting his important interests were to be discussed on the grounds that 'Old Trumpington is such an incompetent chairman that it takes hours to reach a decision'. Conducting and taking part in discussion needs to be learned, and no doubt improves with practice.

As regards employers running 'their own' businesses, the property rules in any society are very much a matter of convention; the kind of 'business' anyone may run and the demands and conditions he may impose on his employees are already highly circumscribed, and the propriety of this is almost universally accepted. Equally, there is no inherent contradiction in the idea of a democratic society deciding democratically that, as in some Eastern bloc countries (Pateman, 1970, pp. 85–102), certain kinds of concern, such as those small undertakings in which the employer works alongside his employees, should be run without formal democratic procedures. The demand for these is most urgent where the employer is remote and impersonal, as in some multinational companies. In such cases there is every danger that decisions adversely affecting workers' interests, or even the way they do their work, will be taken by remote and distant bodies on purely financial grounds, with no knowledge of local conditions and no concern for workers' interests and well-being.

Decisions requiring technical expertise or taken under conditions of urgency pose no insoluble problems for participatory democracy. All of us, however democratic our views, have an interest in such decisions being taken by experts, or being taken promptly as the occasion demands. There are few examples of committed democrats seriously demanding that it should be otherwise. No doubt this is why the unguarded remarks of health service trade unionists and others working in close proximity with acknowledged experts are so eagerly seized upon by participatory democracy's opponents.

## Equality of Influence and Consideration, Democratic Manners and Democratic Values

I noted in Chapter 2 that it was possible to speak of democratic manners or a democratic atmosphere in a community or institution. This, I suggested, might simply denote an easy informality between the different levels of an institution's hierarchy. But it would not seem to be a totally different and separate meaning of the term. Nor is it just a contingent fact that such a style of personal relationships is often observed in democratic societies. The point is rather that this is how one would expect people to behave if they were mutually free and independent and not in any way superior or subordinate to one another. In such a society there are presumed to be no differences of quality or rank to be constantly maintained or acknowledged by one's language and bearing.

Individuals may, of course, be superior or subordinate to each other within the structure of the institutions or organisations to which they belong. Institutions (schools, hospitals, commercial enterprises) may perhaps require a certain strictly functional authority structure in order to be efficient. There is no reason why democrats should not recognise this fact and collectively, even if tacitly, approve of such a structure to meet the requirements of the institution and its aims.

It may even be that the aims and purposes of some institutions, particularly those that work under some pressure of urgency such as armies, hospitals, or police forces, are such that it is important for their members and those with whom they come into contact to be unhesitatingly clear about the level of authority from which instructions or information emanate. In these circumstances it might just be democratically acceptable for people occupying different levels in the functional hierarchy to be constantly reminded of the fact by such things as uniforms, badges of rank, forms of address, and so on.

Styles of personal relations inconsistent with democracy would seem to be those that constantly emphasise such distinctions beyond institutional necessity or imply some general relationship of superiority or subordination between persons. What would above all seem unacceptable are those codes of one-way manners still occasionally found in some educational and other institutions, which constantly imply that only some members of the institution are worthy of courtesy and consideration.

Mention must finally be made of certain so-called democratic values. These are notably freedom, equality and, variously, fraternity, altruism, consideration of interests, and so on. Clearly this last group of values are moral virtues. It may, however, be doubted whether they are necessarily implied by democracy as justified by our mutual independence and non-subordination to each other. Certainly fraternity is an emotional word and it is not obvious that to be committed to democracy is to be committed to going out of one's way to benefit others in normal circumstances.

A society, however, which allows some of its members to be needlessly disadvantaged can scarcely claim to be treating those members as if they were equally entitled to consideration along with others. Much the same may be said of a society which allows some of its members to suffer extreme need or hardship. Both of these situations indicate that the groups in question do not exercise equal influence in collective decisions, for if they did they would see to it that matters were arranged differently.

It is a commonly made point against democracy in practice that those who are unrepresented when decisions are taken are likely to have their interests overlooked. If democracy is justified by a right to equal influence and consideration, then it would seem that this right remains even though a particular group may not be in a position to make its interest felt. In such a case it would seem incumbent upon democrats to act as if those interests were represented, and to protect them

31

accordingly. Such a measure would seem morally obligatory, though by no means a substitute for adequate representation in the long run.

A second contentious issue in the area of democratic values is the supposed conflict between equality and freedom. This largely arises from a misunderstanding. The advocates of freedom as against equality often speak as if egalitarians were concerned to equalise all levels of wealth and life-chances. No doubt there are people who see this as desirable. It is not obvious, however, that differences of wealth as such are inconsistent with the principle of democracy as defined in Chapter 2, providing – and this is an important proviso – that such differences do not enable some people to gain additional power and influence at the expense of others.

Yet it may often be the possibility of gaining additional power and influence over the lives of others that those who demand 'more freedom' and less equality ('the freedom to be unequal') hope to obtain. This, however, is not a general demand for more freedom at all, for in such cases the greater freedom of some will be balanced or exceeded by the greater enslavement of others.

Advocates of equality also need to define their demands clearly if they are not to become incoherent. To impose uniformity in the name of equality may be more irksome to some than to others, for human tastes vary. There is also the problem of who is to do the imposing. For this to be possible an inequality of power must already exist, even if this is only the superior power of the majority who prefer a certain pattern of existence combining to oppress those who do not. The equality that matters to democrats is equality of power and influence, and the differences that concern them are those that are evidence of the lack of such equality, or are detrimental to it.

The equality versus freedom argument arises from a false dichotomy. All that either libertarians or egalitarians may reasonably claim in the name of democracy is equal freedom. From this it follows that no one ought to be coerced except to preserve the freedoms of others and that all ought to have opportunities for the same degree of influence in collective undertakings. This is subject only to the further consequence of equal consideration, that there should be enhanced opportunities to influence decisions in which one's interests are particularly concerned.

# 4

# *Indoctrination, Schooling and Reproduction*

Let us suppose that someone is committed to the democratic view that no one is inherently subordinate to or less important than anyone else. To what views is such a person committed regarding the desirable nature and organisation of education in his society? These are the questions that will concern us in Chapters 5–8. Before turning to these questions, however, it will be helpful to dispose of two lines of argument designed to prevent any such discussion from getting off the ground by showing it to be either improper or pointless. The lines of argument in question are as follows:

(1) Promoting the cause of democracy is a political goal and therefore no part of the teacher's business. Politics should play no part in educational decisions or in the content of education. Teaching for democracy, not to say 'inculcating democratic values', would constitute indoctrination and should therefore be avoided.

(2) Education cannot hope to change society. This is not merely because to bring about such a change would be an enormous undertaking beyond the resources of the school, which cannot hope to compete with the influences of home and the media. More important, far from education affecting the nature of society, it is society and the existing social structure that determine the nature of education. For all the well-intentioned efforts of individual teachers, the educational system as a whole is bound to reproduce the existing power relationships of society. Things could not be otherwise.

The first of these two arguments may be dealt with fairly briefly. The second is a widely influential doctrine which requires examination at some length, and will therefore occupy the bulk of this chapter.

33

## Are Political Aims Inappropriate?

The view that politics should, or even can, be kept out of education is difficult to sustain. In so far as education is the process by which society renews itself and passes on its acquired knowledge and the values it regards as important, it is necessarily political, for the educational experience of the young will affect the future condition of society. This may be expected to happen in two ways.

First, there is the content of education, the actual values, beliefs and knowledge passed on. These may encourage future citizens to be progressive, reactionary, scholarly, practical and many other things besides. Doubts are sometimes cast on the effectiveness of schools, but it would be strange if what was learned in schools were to have no effect on the way pupils came to understand the world and live their lives in society.

Secondly, there is the question of who is taught what. A community might decide, for example, that as far as possible all future citizens ought to have the opportunity of learning more or less the same things. It would also be possible to arrange things so that some were taught a good deal about science, maths and the workings of society, while others were given the rudiments of manual skills and drilled in obedience and docility. Different social and political outcomes might be expected, depending on which course of action were chosen.

Just what content and institutional arrangements one should favour if one is committed to democracy will be discussed in more detail in later chapters. For the present it suffices to establish that such questions cannot be avoided by saying that education and politics are separate activities which should not be mixed.

Many, indeed, of those who are most vociferous in opposing the use of education for what they term 'social engineering' are themselves not entirely free of political motivation and may have an interest in preserving the status quo. To attempt to do so and to intervene in order to prevent educational change taking place is, of course, every bit as political as actively attempting to change things.

A slightly different emphasis is present in the claim that to educate in a way favourable to democracy is necessarily to indoctrinate. This may rest on the more general view that any attempt to influence the beliefs of the young amounts to some sort of indoctrination. On this sort of view, Catholicism, fascism, communism, Islam, monarchism, democracy, and so on, are all beliefs with little to choose between them. If we happen to prefer democracy this is either because it suits our interests, or because we too were indoctrinated or socialised into this preference as children. To attempt to use the educational system to favour democracy is, on this assumption, in no way preferable to the

34

activities of those who at various times have used educational institutions to inculcate other world views.

In replying to this criticism the democrat is bound to argue that liberal democracy is by no means an ideology like its various rivals. On the contrary, whereas the hierarchies in both its religious and its secular alternatives must expend considerable energies in managing information and exerting various kinds of pressure in order to secure orthodoxy, democracy is unique in that it is supposed to thrive on free access to information and open discussion. The democrat is committed to the view that in the long run there is no need to manage information, for the more information is available, the more free-ranging discussion takes place under conditions in which rational argument is possible, the more likely it is that people will come to the conclusion that some form of democracy is the only tolerable form of government.

If free-ranging discussion and access to information lead some pupils to the contrary view, that too must be their right in a democracy. This brings out clearly the difference between the democratic educator and the anti-democratic indoctrinator, for the indoctrinator is, on one widely accepted definition (J. White, 1970), one who is concerned to instil certain substantive beliefs in such a way that they will not later be questioned or changed.

## Does Education Merely Serve to Reproduce Existing Inequalities?

The view that education serves merely to preserve existing inequalities enjoys considerable authority in some parts of the educational world. Some versions of it have been advanced with great dialectical skill and others on the basis of carefully marshalled empirical evidence (Bourdieu and Passeron, 1970; Althusser, 1971).

In essence the argument is as follows. In addition to such crudely repressive 'apparatuses' as the army and the police, the dominant class in any society, that is, the class that controls access to the means of production, has at its disposal various 'ideological apparatuses' such as organised religion, the literary culture, the popular media and, in our own era, the academic world and the educational system. The general function of these is to 'legitimate' the power of the dominant class – that is, to convince the population at large, including most members of the dominant class themselves, that the prevailing order of things is natural and right.

To use the jargon, the repressive state apparatuses (army, police, and so on) which bolster the power of the dominant class by means of physical violence are backed up by the very necessary ideological state apparatuses employing symbolic power, sometimes termed 'symbolic violence'. The message that the ideological state apparatuses put over necessarily serves the interests of the dominant class, for they are materially dependent on that class, as indeed is everyone else.

A slightly different way of looking at the 'ideological state apparatuses', especially schooling, is to see their function as that of keeping 'the capitalist system' supplied with the kind of workers it needs, of 'reproducing' a new lot of workers each generation. Not only must these possess certain skills such as literacy, numeracy and minimum general dexterity; they must also possess certain qualities of character. These may include industriousness and thrift, docility and a readiness to obey instructions without asking too many questions. Above all they must show a willingness to accept that they are suited only to relatively menial tasks, and that anything more complicated is best left to others.

The system may also need to create a certain number of 'cadres', of managerial and supervisory staff who will work to serve the capitalist interest without too much close supervision. This is the function of the progressive education favoured for their own children by many middle-class families, that is, by the parents of many future cadres.

On this kind of view, the point of the content of the curriculum is only partly to furnish working-class children with the skills and information they will later need as workers. Indeed, the workers' needs in this respect have, until recently at least, been very modest. A far more important function of the curriculum, especially the 'high status' or difficult subjects such as maths, foreign languages and physics, is to 'create failure', that is, to create in future workers the view that they are no good at head work or paperwork and are much better suited to working with their hands. If others have more power and earn more money, they are entitled to it because they 'have the brains'. And if some people are very rich indeed, their merits must be correspondingly astronomical.

It is part of this theory that schooling and indeed all ideological state apparatuses not only reproduce an unjust system of social relations but also help to 'mask' or hide the true nature of those relations. Attempts to improve the system or make it 'fairer' by, for instance, making it easier for some working-class children to achieve social mobility are only cosmetic. They do nothing to change the fundamentally repressive structure of society, though they may result in certain roles in that structure being occupied by different individuals. In any case the whole content and ambience of schooling massively discriminates against children from working-class homes because of the greater difference between the culture of their homes and that of the school (Keddie, 1971).

It is therefore pointless, according to this view, to try to change society by such educational means as teaching children to think critically. This would not merely be an uphill struggle that might be won by means of a superhuman effort; it would be doomed from the start. Though usually content to let pedagogues get on with their work without hindrance, representatives of the dominant class would intervene brutally at the first signs that the enterprise of unmasking the true nature of our social relations and thereby of changing those relations stood any chance of being successful.

There is obviously much to be said for such a view of things. Early philanthropists and promoters of education were fairly open in their belief that the provision of education for the poor would both provide better workers and be an aid to social stability and good order (Bowles and Gintis, 1976, pp. 26–36). Economic arguments for providing more resources for education at any level must after all rest on the assumption that education will make people into better workers, or more efficient servants of the administrative superstructure which commercial enterprises need in order to operate.

Whatever the intentions of individual teachers, what goes on in many classrooms predominantly occupied by working-class children is difficult to account for in educational terms. This is true whether we regard education as:

(1)  trying to get children committed to worthwhile activities for their own sake,
(2)  enabling children to understand their own lives and the world about them, so as to be able to make their life-choices rationally, or even as
(3)  the more utilitarian process of equipping children with elementary vocational or life skills.

The watered-down versions of such traditional subjects as history, geography, English, or French as taught to many working-class children can be expected to produce little in the way of either commitment or understanding. Nor do they appear to have a great deal of utilitarian value, certainly little that the children themselves are likely to perceive or make their own. Consequently, it is tempting to interpret what is going on in terms of accustoming children to work at banal, repetitive tasks whose point they do not understand, of being compliant and polite in the case of civilised schools, or of learning to obey peremptory commands promptly in schools that are less civilised.

All three of the educational ideologies mentioned above seem admirably suited to the task of bolstering the existing social order. To suggest that education should be centrally concerned with getting pupils committed to activities which are worthwhile for their own sakes rather than for any instrumental advantage is also an excellent doctrine for gentling not only the masses but also the children of more affluent and ambitious parents. A population committed to intrinsically worthwhile pursuits, whether the high culture of literature, art and music or more homely hobbies such as gardening, pigeon-fancying, or handbell ringing, is less likely to worry about who holds the power in society or how to get a bigger share of society's resources. This will be particularly true if children have acquired the notion that such concerns are rather vulgar.

The idea of bringing children to an understanding of the world in which they live so that they can make rational life-choices has similar potential for concealing people's true situation from them. This approach may create the illusion, perhaps in some cases even the reality, of individual freedom. Here is the individual furnished with a knowledge of the world and of the various values a human being may pursue. All he has to do now, apparently, is to choose the way of life that seems best to him.

Of course, most individuals are in no position to do anything of the kind. They may perhaps have some choice in such marginal matters as how, within rather narrow limits, they will spend their evenings and weekends, or how they will use whatever surplus income they may have after basic needs have been met. For the most part, however, they will have little choice about how they will spend the major part of their waking lives, namely their working hours.

Even those who do to some extent choose their occupation or way of life do so within a range of options made available to them by the existing social and occupational structure. At the outside it might just be argued that almost anyone who really wants to can be an archbishop, or a managing director, or a Member of Parliament. Just conceivably those who think they want these things but do not achieve them did not really want them at all, and had other priorities in life. But in the end only a certain number of individuals can achieve dominant positions in a hierarchical society. What the ideology of individual freedom does is to buy people off with the hope of achieving their aspirations, without endangering the existing structure.

Finally, the doctrine of vocational relevance or usefulness serves the existing structure in a much cruder and more obvious way. Besides providing some technical skills, education for a particular occupational role suggests that that role is both appropriate to the individuals being prepared for it and a natural and fairly permanent feature of the universe. Someone who has painstakingly acquired the prerequisites of even a relatively lowly occupation and become identified with the status that goes with it already has a vested interest in preserving the present state of society.

In the doctrine that education's main function is to legitimate present inequality, an important part is played by educational assessment. In some occupations, such as bus driving, architecture, or dentistry, certificates of competence are a convenient way of protecting the public by ensuring that the practitioner has followed a suitable course of instruction. For many occupations, however, as well as for progression to higher stages of education, a minimum *number* of examination subjects passed is often a necessary qualification. This gives support to the contention that examination requirements are being used purely as a rationing device, and that the actual learning that precedes the examinations is largely irrelevant.

Further support is given to this contention by the fact that most examinations taken by school pupils are 'norm based' rather than 'criterion based'. Pass marks are fixed not in relation to a particular standard of achievement but in relation to a set proportion of the candidates entered. Possibly too much importance should not be attached to this point, since in practice the quality of candidates taking a particular examination is only likely to vary slightly from year to year. Examination requirements for entry into various occupations and various institutions of higher education may, however, be raised and lowered with comparative ease.

The scientific and predictive shortcomings of various kinds of educational assessment and labelling, and especially the notion of a fixed IQ, are well documented and do not centrally concern us here. Empirical investigators have also come to some understanding of the various ways in which children from less privileged backgrounds are prevented from achieving social and educational mobility. Doubtless teacher expectation and home/school differences in language and styles of motivation, not to mention a measure of sheer teacher prejudice, all play their part.

It was earlier suggested that even if educators succeeded in promoting a more critical attitude towards our social arrangements, those who hold power in our society would simply not allow such a spirit to develop. Recent events may seem to provide evidence for this view. The political ferment in educational institutions during the late 1960s and early 1970s has certainly been followed by a pronounced swing towards tougher attitudes and tighter control. Financial cuts have enabled 'trouble-makers' and 'ineffective teachers' to be shown the real possibility of being out of a job. At the level of higher education such cuts have fallen with particular severity on the social science disciplines which have been most productive of criticism of the existing order.

## Education as Oppression – Some Reservations

So is it, then, really true that the teacher who is committed to democracy or any just form of social order has no alternative but to take to the streets and foment revolution? Is it really the case that by trying to teach in a way appropriate to future citizens of a democracy, or by pressing for more democratic educational policies, he is simply playing into the hands of 'anti-democratic forces' by providing palliatives or helping to mask the true situation?

Though it is difficult to deny many of the criticisms of the current educational situation set out above, a number of reservations are to be made if the activities of teachers and the nature of educational institutions are to be seen in perspective. An important feature of the doctrine we have been considering is the fact that it more or less deliberately ignores both the value of what is learned in schools and the intentions and understandings of teachers and others working in the educational system. There do, of course, exist attractive and quite well established lines of justification for such an approach. On some hard-line empiricist views, talk of values is no more than the expression of personal preference and is to be avoided by serious thinkers as unscientific. Alternatively, it may be argued that since the values of a society simply reflect the interests of the dominant class, writers are quite right to discount them when discussing education or any other social phenomenon.

The intentions of teachers and their understanding of what they are doing may likewise be dismissed as intangible and not properly accessible to rigorous study, if not actually misguided or subject to the delusions of false consciousness. Far better to stick to the 'objective facts' about the actual social effects of what teachers do. Such arguments naturally have a good deal of easy appeal to professional debunkers, since they allow the whole of the existing system and many of the arguments that might be used to defend it to be dismissed at a single stroke. The rhetoric of iconoclasm is easily grasped and used. If all educational endeavour is to be condemned, careful distinctions between the valid and the invalid need not be made, and arguments that cannot be refuted may simply be held up as evidence of the speaker's stubbornness and bad faith.

To ignore the intentions and understandings of teachers and the values and achievements they see themselves as attempting to pass on is, however, to take a limited view of education, and of human activity generally. Discussion of human activities which fails to take account of the agents' values, intentions and purposes – the concepts by which they make sense of what they do – fails to do justice to the specifically human quality of those activities (see Winch, 1958, pp. 68–94; Harré and Secord, 1972, pp. 101–24). Thus, while it may be perfectly appropriate to point to the many undesirable side-effects of what teachers and the educational system do, we may not refuse to take seriously what teachers say their intentions are in teaching the various subjects of the curriculum, or in insisting on acceptable modes of behaviour.

Likewise it may certainly be true that pupils' progress in various academic fields may serve to sort people into different occupational categories. This, however, does not justify our entirely discounting the positive value of what pupils learn of mathematics, the arts, the physical and indeed the social sciences. Of course, the side-effects in terms of legitimation and possible social injustice are also part of the picture and in the end we might want to say that these outweigh the value of the world's present cultural achievements and of passing them on in schools. That point of view is certainly an option that mankind may eventually choose. But to see education and the transmission of existing knowledge and understanding as nothing more than a device of legitimation and oppression is to suppress one half of the equation.

There is a further intellectual shortcoming in the view that schooling necessarily cements existing inequalities, and therefore cannot be used as a means of removing some of them. This is the fact that any theory that claims that something 'must' be the case is automatically suspect. It is especially suspect if criticisms of it tend to be met not with argument but with accusations that the critic is too contemptibly naïve to merit a reply, or has in some way sold out to the class enemy. The claim that something 'must' be the case is not a scientific or empirical claim at all. For if something must be the case, then whatever evidence is brought to light it will make no difference to the conclusion.

Thus if schools are found to be authoritarian, this is taken as fairly straightforward evidence for the sort of theory we have been discussing. Such schools are clearly inculcating docility and compliance. But if schools are found to be liberal and to encourage active participation and questioning, this too is held to be evidence for the theory. Such schools are either held to be engaged in some more subtle form of socialisation into acceptance of the status quo, or they are supposed to be part of the process by which the true nature of the situation is concealed.

One may therefore quite properly ask what would count as evidence against the theory. The answer is that nothing would. Whatever was found to be the case would receive an interpretation that would favour rather than falsify the theory. In much the same way some religious fundamentalists see the geological evidence for evolution as just one more proof of the devil's cunning in tricking humanity into false beliefs.

It is important that we should be quite clear what is here being argued. It is readily conceded that as a matter of fact the educational system as we have it is massively biased in favour of preserving an unequal and morally quite unacceptable social structure. To believe that something just is the case, however, is quite different from accepting that whatever one does, it absolutely must be so. It is also more helpful to the teacher seeking guidance as to how he should approach his work in the classroom.

Once it is accepted that things might be different from the way they are, the question 'What ought the teacher to do?' becomes a cue for reasoned and critical discussion, rather than derision or despair. It still has to be shown that anything the individual can do will have any effect, but at least the question of whether some actions or policies are preferable to others is no longer without point.

It may, of course, turn out that the individual is relatively powerless. But this should not be too readily assumed. As a present or future qualified teacher, the reader will certainly have some latitude over what he does and how. Even if he is a relatively docile individual, generally inclined to do as he is bid, he still has the choice between dragging his feet over plainly anti-democratic policies, and leaping to implement them with odious zeal. As he moves up the hierarchy, he will certainly be in a position to increase at least marginally the amount of control some people have over their own lives and activities, or to prevent such control from being eroded.

If such marginal improvements seem trifling and not greatly to affect the grand structure of society, two points are to be made. First, such small changes in the everyday experience of pupils and teachers may be subjectively more important to them than seeing the whole social structure overturned. Secondly, even the slightest taste of independence may prove addictive. Revolutions may not be made by the utterly oppressed, but by those who have acquired the taste and expectation of liberty.

Opponents of this view will be quick to castigate it as 'gradualism'. Small changes, it may be implied, give the illusion of progress, but never amount to much, and democratic freedoms granted from above may always be taken away. It has not, however, been convincingly shown that gradual changes may not be cumulative. Even if it is thought that the individual by himself is unable to achieve a great deal, this does not mean that his efforts are bound to be useless. Among other things, democracy is necessarily about attempting to change things in co-operation with others.

The teacher who is committed to the values of democracy will certainly find resonances in the aspirations of some of his colleagues. It is not even obvious that all those in positions of power and authority in the educational system are committed to preserving the status quo. Many, indeed, seem fuelled by quite the opposite desire, even allowing for a generous measure of hypocrisy and self-deception.

# 5

# Equality, Freedom and Diversity

In Chapter 4 we considered and rejected arguments to the effect that promoting democracy through educational institutions was inappropriate or impossible. The way is now clear to consider the implications of a commitment to the democratic ideal we have elaborated for the organisation and content of education. The organisation of particular educational institutions and the content of education appropriate in a democracy will be considered in Chapters 6, 7 and 8. The present chapter is principally concerned with the distribution of educational opportunities.

In Chapter 3 it was argued that there are no good reasons for thinking that any one person's interests and aspirations are more important than those of anyone else. From this it was concluded that ideally things should be arranged to ensure that as far as possible all come to have equal chances of controlling their own lives and influencing the conduct of the community's joint undertakings. If this argument is accepted, it would seem to follow that various institutions in the community ought to favour, or at least not obstruct, the realisation of these aims.

Until quite recently it was widely assumed that both academic selection for separate schools within the state system and the existence of private education were more or less indefensible, being contrary to the principle of 'equality of opportunity'. Such arrangements, it was held, produced different types or categories of citizen, and enabled some to accede to a range of better life-chances, including better chances of controlling their own lives and influencing the community's common undertakings, than others.

It was no doubt supposed that some people might make a last-ditch stand in defence of both selection and private education. Such defences were rarely taken seriously, however, and it was expected that eventually both selection and, after a somewhat longer period, private schooling would cease to exist, or be reduced to insignificant proportions. More recently, however, sustained argument (Cooper, 1975, 1980) has been put forward in favour of mixed-quality education within the state system. There has also been considerable support (Friedman, 1962, pp. 85–107; West, 1970) not only for the retention but also for the encouragement and expansion of private schooling.

It has been suggested by a defender of both selection and private schooling (Cooper, 1980, pp. 67–75) that the term 'equality of opportunity' has been so variously and confusingly used as to have become meaningless and therefore unserviceable in educational discussion. This is not so. The notion has been and remains an important one in discussing the politics of educational distribution. If the term is used in a number of ways it is possible to distinguish between them, and the making of these distinctions is worth undertaking, since it raises a number of important issues of principle.

## Democracy and Equality of Opportunity

The first distinction to be made under the heading of equality of opportunity is that drawn by Crosland (1962, pp. 169–78) between what he terms 'strong' and 'weak' versions of the principle. According to the weak version, equality of educational opportunity might have been said ideally to exist under some such competitive system as the old 11-plus examination. Under such a system properly operated, all children would have the chance to compete for access to education of higher quality and longer duration on the basis of their current knowledge and abilities.

In fact, of course, the 11-plus did not even bring about equality of educational opportunity in this weak sense, for a child's chances of access to a selective school depended not only on his knowledge and ability but also on the geographical distribution of grammar school places. It is also possible that some selection procedures involving such things as primary school teachers' recommendations and grammar school headmasters' interviews may have given an unfair advantage to some children, in the perfectly banal sense that a part may have been played by favouritism or graft.

But even supposing such unfairnesses to have been eliminated, this kind of competition for access to higher-quality schools on the basis of existing attainments and abilities would not satisfy the requirements of Crosland's strong concept of equality of opportunity. In sitting an examination at 11-plus or whatever age, some children will already have a significant advantage over others, however scrupulously the papers are marked and however evenly grammar school places are distributed. Children's test performance will be affected both by the previous schooling the child has received and by his home background. Despite the efforts of those engaged in test construction, no one has yet come up with a test that is universally accepted as measuring innate ability unaffected by experience. Even if this were possible, it would still be open to question whether someone ought to be offered an inferior educational experience, and consequently inferior life-chances, on the basis of some innate characteristic over which he had no control. The strong concept of equality of opportunity requires that, in Crosland's words, all should have 'an equal chance to acquire intelligence' (p. 123). At very least such a concept would seem to imply that where access to education of a superior kind was competitive, every effort should be made to ensure that all were equal at the starting-line.

This requirement would not be met, however objective the admission test, if some children were at a disadvantage because they had failed to acquire certain attainments or certain attitudes to school work because of their previous education or home background. Needless to say, it is now well established that many working-class children bring from their home background two important disadvantages. First, the range of language they experience and are encouraged to use will be less extensive and less likely to be helpful to them at school than that experienced by middle-class children. Secondly, they will be less convinced of the value of doing well at school and receive less encouragement in this respect. This is not to say (or to deny) that working-class language or working-class attitudes are in any way inferior or any less valid than those of other social groups. It is merely that they are less helpful to a child in school. Equally, it is not being said that all working-class children are at a disadvantage in this regard compared with all middle-class children. This is just the way it works out on average.

The old-fashioned IQ test which often formed a major part of 11-plus selection instruments was intended to minimise any unfairness that might arise from differences in previous learning. Such tests were rarely, if ever, the only kind of test to be used. Few people now believe that IQ remains stable throughout an individual's life, or is unaffected by a child's previous experience.

Furthermore, even if some children are innately less clever than others it is not clear that a democrat should regard this as a reason for devoting less resources to those children's early experience and education. On the contrary, it might be argued with equal conviction that everything possible should be done to counteract the inequalities of nature rather than accentuate them.

On extreme interpretations, the requirement of equality of

educational opportunity is taken to mean not merely that all children should receive the benefit of the same quantity of educational resources, but that outcomes should be equal. It is not clear whether this means that all children should emerge from school or university knowing the self-same things, or just roughly the same amount of things.

If it is thought that this requirement is a bit steep, some writers (e.g. Robinson, 1981, p. 155) propose a less stringent, compromise criterion which is nevertheless stronger than the mere demand that educational inputs should be equal. According to this criterion, equality of educational opportunity exists when the proportion of the population having certain non-educational characteristics (red hair, feminine sex, working-class parents, and so on) is the same at any educational level as it is in the population as a whole. Thus, for example, if approximately half the population is female, then equality of opportunity between men and women exists if half the sixth-formers and university entrants are girls, girls take half the Firsts, half the PhDs, and of course half the Thirds, and so on. Likewise, if one in nine of the population were to have red hair or black skin then we should expect about one in nine of the Oxbridge Firsts, or whatever, to be red-haired or black-skinned also. Any marked difference requires some explanation. If no genetic link can be found between, say, red hair and mental inability, then maybe prejudice against red hair exists among those who select for entry to the higher stages of the education system. Or possibly the explanation may lie in some element in the socialisation process which leads those with the characteristic in question to regard a high level of educational achievement as inappropriate to them.

It is, however, not absolutely clear whether writers who adopt this 'group representation' version of equality of educational opportunity regard such proportionality as the necessary evidence of equality of opportunity, or as a definition of it. That is to say, it is not clear whether they are simply saying that in the absence of any other acceptable explanation, differences in distribution prove that some form of bias has been operative in the selection system, or whether they are saying that the principle of equality of opportunity requires that the proportion of women, blacks, Jehova's Witnesses, and so on, achieving various educational outcomes should be the same as in society as a whole, irrespective of any inherent differences that may exist between the members of those groups.

So far we have distinguished between a number of possible and perfectly comprehensible interpretations of the term 'equality of educational opportunity'. It is difficult to see how such a notion can lightly be dismissed from discussion of how education should be distributed in any community that claims to be a democracy. It has been argued that a democracy is a society in which opportunities for power and influence are, as far as possible, equally distributed. One important route to power and influence in our society is through the educational system.

This being so, it would seem that the very least the democrat can aim at is the removal of a situation in which some people are from the outset debarred from certain influential positions because there is no realistic possibility of their receiving the necessary education. If this is accepted, it is difficult to see how a democrat could find any set-up acceptable which did not ensure both Crosland's weak and strong forms of equality of opportunity. Indeed, if it is the case that power and influence are necessarily tied to educational attainment, then it is hard to see how democrats can stop short of demanding that teachers should work for equality of outcomes in so far as that is a feasible proposition. Whether or not this could be done by concentrating a great deal of care and effort on the teaching and encouragement of children from the least favoured backgrounds is largely an empirical question.

An alternative possibility would, of course, be to urge that we should do our utmost to reduce educational inequality by a policy of levelling down – that is, by holding back the able or talented child, or at least not going out of one's way to provide him with stimulus or instruction until the least gifted or least motivated have caught up with him.

Such levelling down is rarely proposed by serious egalitarians, though it is sometimes ascribed to them by their opponents. It is not, however, an obvious absurdity to stop encouraging, or even to hold back, an otherwise admirable talent if it is in some way destructively divisive of society or grossly humiliating to others, or consumes resources vital to other people's basic well-being. Talent is but one value among many, and there is no reason why it should always be favoured at the expense of other values.

Seen from another point of view, however, democrats have perhaps sometimes been needlessly unwary in condemning intellectual and cultural elites. In intellectual and cultural elites *per se* there would appear to be little harm. Normally, indeed, all except those incurably infected with envy are able to delight in the achievements – especially the exceptional achievements – of others, whether these are the result of innate ability, dedicated teaching, or personal effort. Frequently, too, all may materially benefit from the abilities and talents of others. In such cases all may, in accordance with Rawls's difference principle (Rawls, pp. 75–83), be expected to approve of extra resources being devoted to their cultivation. It is also difficult to see how anyone could disapprove of an educational system that permitted and encouraged the development of a range of talents, if this led to no more than harmless diversity.

What must be objectionable to the democrat, however, is the situation in which differing educational achievements systematically reinforce existing social and political stratification, or are the basis of new forms of stratification which have not existed previously. To a democrat, a stratified or hierarchical society is offensive whether based on birth, wealth, or differences of educational experience and achievement. No doubt some injustices would have been removed if more working-class boys or more coloured women were able to aspire to the highest academic honours and subsequently to distinguished professional or political careers. It is not abundantly clear, however, that any great gain would have been made from the democrat's point of view if the structure of society remained the same, with only the identity of those occupying the dominant roles being changed.

It is in the light of these considerations that we now turn to questions raised by 'mixed-quality state education' (selection within the state system) and the existence and promotion of private schooling.

## Mixed-Quality State Education

David Cooper's *Illusions of Equality* (1980) achieved something of a *succès de scandale* by arguing that it is justifiable to have mixed-quality education within the state system, that is, a selective system of state education in which more resources are devoted to the education of the ablest children. Such a system, Cooper holds, would be justified even if it brought no benefit to the least well off members of society, and even if the least well educated children were worse educated than in a system in which educational resources were distributed equally.

The most convincing part of Cooper's critique of egalitarian arguments about education is where he claims that much polemical writing which purports to be about educational inequality is not about educational inequality at all. He refers to writers who contrast the education given in, say, an inner city comprehensive school with that received in one of the more favoured public schools. While conceding that the education given in the city centre school gives cause for concern, Cooper claims that the issue is not one of inequality, for the bad education given in the comprehensive school would be a reason for improving things irrespective of what goes on in more favoured places.

One cannot fail to agree with Cooper's claim that many of the statistics that are supposed to demonstrate educational inequality are not concerned with educational inequality at all but with the social inequalities to which various groups are subject after they leave school.

In an attempt to distinguish the issue of specifically educational inequality from related but separate issues, Cooper describes the educational system of an imaginary state which he calls Scholesia. An important feature of this state is that except in the field of education it embodies the supposed principle of social justice, that only those inequalities are allowed that are beneficial to the least fortunate. In the field of education, however, mixed-quality selective education is provided. The ablest 20 per cent or so of the population receive a more expensive and higher-quality education than the rest, despite the fact that the rest will receive a less good education in consequence.

Cooper's purpose in constructing such a simplified model of an educational system is to consider whether educational inequality as such is morally unacceptable when the question is considered in isolation from other supposed injustices that seem to accompany educational inequality in the real world. To this end it is specified in the model that the education of the less able 80 per cent of the population is not grossly neglected. Selection for 'North', the school of the more able pupils, is 'fair' in the sense that it is based on accurately tested ability and that though more educated parents tend to have more able children, such parents are not necessarily richer than other members of the population. Nor does having been at North lead to people being materially better off in later life, though it is conceded that they may later do jobs for which their better education particularly suits them.

Having shown, as he claims, that such an unequal distribution of educational goods is not only permissible but actually desirable, Cooper then considers individually various effects of educational inequality in real life to see whether these give us grounds for saying that mixed-quality education is undesirable in the real world. His conclusion is that such a system constitutes no injustice either in the theoretical model state of Scholesia or in the real world.

It is, perhaps, a mistake to take all this too seriously. One of the general difficulties experienced in dealing with Cooper's work is the apparent tongue-in-cheek quality of many of his arguments. In consequence one is often faced with the choice of letting past an argument that is clearly defective or revealing oneself to be a humourless boor by responding too earnestly to what was intended as a nonchalant throw-away. Nevertheless, it is proposed to go some way in following John and Pat White who point to what seem to be some of the main shortcomings in Cooper's argument (White and White, 1980).

Principal among these is the fact that Cooper takes it for granted that there is a prima-facie case for adopting that educational system among the various alternatives which most approximates towards an ideal of excellence in educational standards (Cooper, 1980, p. 53). He also makes it clear that the improvement he is concerned with is what he terms an 'ontological' improvement rather than a distributional one. He is concerned, that is, that some people should be educated better than anyone was educated before, rather than that the average standard should be raised. This, he claims (p. 55), is the natural context of our talk of rising or falling standards:

> The prime concern of the lover of music or athletics is not with a general or marginal improvement in the amateur playing of string quartets, or the times clocked by run-of-the-mill club runners; but with seeing the highest standards of musicianship maintained or advanced, with seeing great athletes break new barriers. Indeed it is hard to see how otherwise he can count as a real lover of music or athletics.

Or again (p. 54):

> If English football is in decline, this is not because fourth division clubs are playing worse than ever, but because the top teams, and the national team, are not playing as well as of yore.

To accept this is, of course, to sell the pass, for it is part of Cooper's definition of his selective 'North–South' model of an educational system that some people will be better educated in this system than at 'Centre' in which educational goods are more evenly distributed.

Even taking Cooper's chosen examples of music and sport, however, it is not clear that a true lover of these activities would necessarily be concerned with the outstanding performances of champions and virtuosi rather than with there being a good level of interest, participation and competence in the community as a whole. For Cooper simply to maintain that he will is for him to be already committed to the position for which he is arguing.

Cooper's case becomes even shakier if we draw our comparison from certain other kinds of excellence. Suppose we were concerned with standards of moral conduct or health care, for example. If banditry were fairly widespread, and those of ordinary constitution were often left to rot with infection, it would be no consolation to be told, 'Ah yes, we distribute our resources so that at least *some* people are fitter and more saintly than before. Ontologically speaking, standards are rising.'

It is also curious if Cooper is concerned with ontological excellence that he should also seem to regard it as a competitive, that is, a distributional term. For according to Cooper, excellence logically requires, not that one should do something extremely well, but that one should do it better than anyone else. He quotes Nietzsche's attack on 'egalitarian tarantulas' (p. 56):

> Life wants to build itself up into the heights with pillars and steps;

50

it wants to look into vast distances and out towards stirring beauties: therefore it requires height. And because it requires height, it requires steps and contradiction among the steps and the climbers.

From this it would almost seem that excellence in the few is logically to be achieved by holding down the level of the rest!

But weaknesses are to be found not only in Cooper's attempt to justify the imaginary educational system of Scholesia but also in the impossibility of its application to the real world. Scholesian children are allocated between North and South by means of infallible tests. In the real world there is no universal consensus as to what constitute the most valuable educational achievements. Disagreement is always possible since the weighting of values is involved. So there can be no final or authoritative pronouncement of such matters. Beside this it is a small point that as a matter of fact we have no infallible tests. When tests are fallible, unfairnesses may arise even though no deliberate wrong-doing may be involved.

Even in Scholesia, old Northites may not earn more money but they have a nicer life in terms of the values Scholesians hold. In the real world it is impossible to see how ex-Northites could be dissuaded or prevented from converting their superiority in knowledge, understanding of society, articulacy and other advantages acquired at the expense of society as a whole into power and cash. Such a group no doubt would, indeed often *do*, see themselves as justified in 'devoting special attention and giving special encouragement, special opportunities and special rewards' (p. 46) to their own children and protecting them from contact with working-class children who are, it is implied, crude and lacking in gentility (p. 96) if not actually repulsive (p. 95).

There is nothing in the education of such a group, either in the content of their curriculum or the social exclusiveness of their schooling, to prevent their seeing themselves as 'special', as having special merits and special deserts – a minority, but a substantial minority, with special achievements and common values, common experience and, above all, common interests to defend against the remainder of society. In short, it is difficult to imagine how such a group are to be prevented from seeing themselves as a special class, an elite of power, prestige and influence. To argue, as Cooper does (pp. 46–9), that they are not in some other (e.g. military) sense an elite is to throw dust in the eyes of honest inquiry.

As a conclusion to this section it is important to stress what seems to be the great value of Cooper's work. This lies in the exposure of the many slipshod and self-indulgent arguments which egalitarians have

51

allowed themselves in the past, and which have brought their case somewhat into disrepute. On the positive side, however, Cooper's case for unequal educational provision remains an entertaining *tour de force* rather than a convincing argument, either in its pure form in the imaginary state of Scholesia or in its application to reality.

For as long as access to power and influence is linked to educational experience, anyone committed to democracy must remain suspicious of any proposal which will result in a significant section of the population receiving a special and recognisably superior form of education. This applies both to provision within the state system and to the encouragement of any system of private education operating alongside a minimal and increasingly ill-endowed public provision for the majority of future citizens. The arguments concerning private education are, however, rather different from those favouring unequal state provision and may be thought more substantial and difficult to refute. They therefore require to be treated separately.

## Private Education in a Democracy

It has to be admitted that the adherent of democracy as I have developed the term in earlier chapters must find the question of private education something of an embarrassment. On the one hand, there does seem to be something rather undemocratic about the present situation. The ex-pupils of certain schools do seem to be at a competitive advantage as far as their life-chances are concerned, particularly when it comes to gaining power and influence over both their own lives and those of others. There is an undeniable preponderance of the ex-pupils of some private schools in government, and in the leading positions in financial, academic and religious institutions, as well as in the worlds of art, literature, journalism and the other media. This does not even have the meritocratic justification that selective schooling based on ability may be said to have. Even children of relatively modest abilities are admitted to major independent schools if their parents can afford to pay the fees and are aware of the importance of putting their names down sufficiently early.

There seems much force in the claim that allowing the powerful and articulate to buy out of the public system leads to falling standards in that system. The powerful are less ready to defend a system to which their own children are not subject. Indeed, many of the most vigorous defenders of private education are also strong advocates of cuts in public (including educational) spending.

However, as soon as the democrat urges the abolition of private schooling he is assailed by a number of arguments which appear to be of unimpeachably democratic lineage and even to be implied by the very principles upon which he stands. In recent years it has been argued that these not only support the continuation of private education but also require that it should be encouraged and subsidised. Writers of both right and left (Friedman, 1962; Illich, 1971) have advocated the issue of vouchers that would enable individuals to purchase instruction from the source of their choice. The authority of J. S. Mill has been claimed (Cohen, 1981, p. 16) for the view that though the state should take steps to ensure that everyone actually receives an adequate education, a state monopoly of educational provision should be avoided.

The principal arguments against the abolition of private education which it is proposed to discuss are the following:

(1)   To abolish private schools or forcibly absorb them into the state system would in many cases be to destroy excellence.
(2)   Such a step would curtail the liberty of the individual and take away his ability to spend his own money as he pleases. There appears to be an inconsistency in allowing parents to provide other educational experiences (books, trips abroad, swimming lessons) for their children while preventing them from retaining the services of better-than-average teachers.
(3)   The abolition of private education would infringe the human right of parents to bring up their own children as they wish.
(4)   It would create a state monopoly in education and lead to drab conformity and totalitarianism.

## Destroying Excellence

It does seem that certain private schools are good schools by any reasonable standards. Their pupils come out well integrated, socially competent, humane, enlightened and public-spirited – and get good A levels into the bargain. The opponent of private schooling does his case no good if he denies this. Nor is it necessary to hold that the superior educational outcomes of these schools are entirely accounted for by the superior native abilities of the pupils, or their more favourable home backgrounds. It is at least reasonable to suppose that these are in part the result of the better qualifications and greater dedication of staff, as well as of superior resources. These may include better teacher/pupil ratios, more aesthetically tolerable buildings, better-stocked libraries and better-equipped science laboratories. Such schools offer staff salaries rather above the average, as well as attractive conditions of work.

While private schools exist funds are likely to be available to enable them just to have the edge on their state rivals and to give their pupils a small but significant margin of advantage in any educationally competitive situation in later life. It is difficult to see how such schools can be priced out of the market while a wide discrepancy of parental incomes remains.

If excellence were a comparative term as has been suggested (see above, page 51) the abolition of private schools would not matter too much, since the best of the remaining (i.e. state) schools would come to be considered excellent in their place. This would be true whether or not the staff and resources of private schools were directly transferred to the state system, which must be admitted to be unlikely.

It is not proposed, however, to rely on the argument that excellence is comparative, for it does seem that something of absolute value may be lost when an effective educational institution is closed or has its character radically changed. What seems a more honest and quite acceptable approach is for the democrat to concede that this loss may be the price he has to pay if the principles he holds are put into practice.

He may, of course, hope that if private schooling were no longer available, the more powerful and articulate members of society would accept the logic of the fact that the level of their own children's education could only be raised by improving the education of all. Only thus is it remotely likely that the education of all will be adequately resourced. The even temporary loss of excellence must necessarily be regretted, but in matters of government hard decisions between interests and values may sometimes have to be made.

## The Freedom of the Individual

It is sometimes suggested that the principle of equality is but one value among others. Other values may be taken to include such things as the promotion of excellence, the privacy and integrity of the family and the principle of freedom. These are all supposed to be absolutely incommensurable values that must be weighed and balanced in such a way that morally acceptable decisions take due account of all of them.

This view that there exists such a set of mutually independent and separately apprehended values is known as intuitionism. It has the disadvantages that it provides no means of adjudicating between values and that any individual's judgement as to what weight should be allocated to which values is beyond criticism. In consequence, when someone asserts that certain institutions ought to be abolished in the name of equality of access to influence and power, he is liable to be met by the counter-claim that they should be preserved in the name of other, incommensurable values.

If he claims to believe in democracy, he is also likely to be told that as a democrat he ought to concede that other people's intimations and aspirations should be allowed equal standing with his own. If, therefore, he wishes to work for democracy and equality in some schools, then he must in justice allow others to pursue other values, such as freedom, including the freedom to be unequal, elsewhere.

This seems a bizarre perversion of the relationship between values, particularly between the supposedly democratic values of equality and freedom. It is true that, as we saw in Chapter 3, our justification of democracy implies both equality and freedom. As we also saw, however, democratic freedom and democratic equality are mutually interdependent. They are not independently intuited incommensurables which must each be allowed 'reasonable weight' or, to put it less mysteriously, between which the individual may choose as it suits his purposes without the possibility of effective challenge.

The problem is – and herein lies the fallacy – that the freedom to educate privately does not seem to interfere with anyone else's freedom to do anything at all. Education is apparently not a zero-sum game. The supply of teachers and resources is relatively elastic and child A's private education does not seem to prevent child B from receiving the same. Sometimes it is even argued that by educating his child privately A's parent leaves more public resources available for the education of child B if B's parents cannot afford private education. As we saw above, however, A's being able to opt out into the private sector is more likely to mean that B will get a worse education in the state system.

There is a further point. Education is not a finite resource for which we are all in competition. If one pupil receives more education, this does not necessarily mean that there will be less of it for others. The same, however, is not true of power and influence. If some people have more power and influence, this can only be at the expense of others who have less. The objection to private schools is not that their pupils receive a better education as such. Anti-egalitarians may try to pretend that that is the objection, and feign puzzlement as to how such an objection can be justified. The real objection is that the ex-pupils of some schools seem to end up with more than their fair share of power and influence; in other words, the objection is to the social effect of private schools in creating a kind of two-tier society, made up of two relatively easily distinguishable kinds of people, some of whom have easier access to favoured positions than others. It is not really so puzzling that this should give rise to complaint in a democracy.

The claim that the abolition of private education would take away the individual's right to spend his own money in ways of his own choosing is an emotive and superficial one. There are many things we are not allowed to do with our own money and our own property if these things have undesirable social consequences. The fact that opponents of private schools do not seem to object to parents buying books or laying on other educational experiences such as theatre visits and swimming lessons for their children is not an inconsistency as is sometimes said. It is, rather, a clear indication that it is not that some children are in a position to learn more than others that is objectionable, but the social side-effects of private schools as institutions.

## The Right to Bring Up One's Children as One Chooses

Nothing seems more natural, more reasonable and more in keeping with an enlightened democracy than that parents should be free to bring up their children in their own way, according to their own traditions, beliefs and values. Though the state may be expected to ensure that individual children do not suffer corruption or neglect, the picture of an authoritarian state compulsorily taking children from their parents and subjecting them to educational experiences and views that are philosophically obnoxious or scandalous to their religious beliefs is not one which a democrat would find it agreeable to have to defend. Parents may be thought to be the people most likely to have their children's best interests at heart, and sensitive and educated parents may reasonably be expected to be good judges of where their children's best interests lie.

The privacy and integrity of the family and the right of parents to choose the kind of education that shall be given to their children also receive support from such widely respected international documents as the *International Covenant on Economic Social and Cultural Rights* (Articles 3, 4, 13), the *European Covenant for the Protection of Human Rights and Fundamental Freedoms* (Protocol, Article 2) and especially the *Universal Declaration of Human Rights* of which Article (iii) reads 'Parents have a prior right to choose the kind of education that shall be given to their children'.

How is the democrat to respond to such arguments in the mouths of the supporters of institutions which seem to him fairly anti-democratic in their social effects? The most likely if highly regrettable answer would seem to be, with exasperation at his constant failure to find a supporter of private education who will take seriously the issue of the social effects of a group of highly effective, prestigeful and influential schools to which entry is virtually restricted to those whose parents belong or aspire to a particular, fairly closely knit social stratum. Can there really be a human right to profit from inequality?

No one but a bigot or an obsessive totalitarian would wish to prevent a parent from making private arrangements for his children's education if all that was involved was a desire to bring up one's children according to one's religious beliefs, or philosophical and educational principles, fostering one's children's artistic, literary, or intellectual gifts, or even

56

an over-solicitous desire to protect one's tender offspring from the traumatic encounter (Bantock, 1975, p. 141) with children from other backgrounds. Private schools, especially the country's major private schools, do not simply provide a haven for those who find the pedagogy, curriculum content and values of the state system unpalatable.

Doubtless there are parents (Cohen, 1981, pp. 25–35) who are sincere in their rejection of the kinds of education the state offers for reasons of the kind mentioned above, unconnected with any desire to preserve a stratified society in which they and their friends and families occupy the more favoured positions. If this is so there would seem no reason why anyone should object to their arranging for the private and specialised education of their children, if this were done in modest, uninfluential institutions which did not distort the social structure or confer special material advantages on their children.

Anyone genuinely concerned with freedom of choice through private education ought to distance himself from the traditional private schools which make the abolition of private education a tempting and legitimate objective to political parties with a special commitment to social justice.

## State Monopoly, Totalitarianism and Drab Conformity

A slightly different slant to the question of private education is given by those who, taking support from Mill, feel that private education should not only be allowed but actually encouraged, even to the point where all education is privately provided.

Such writers often have a general commitment to the reduction of state provision in all fields and argue that freedom of choice and quality of service are maximised when dissatisfied clients are free to take their custom elsewhere. Limiting state activity in all fields is seen as a move against totalitarianism. In education it is seen as particularly important not to allow the state anything like a monopoly in the supply and certification of knowledge as this favours political indoctrination.

Not only does a state monopoly of education favour political abuse, it is also liable to lead to drab conformity and standardisation. It is claimed (West, 1970, pp. 111–73) that in the past even families of modest means in Britain made fairly acceptable private arrangements for the education of their children and that this trend would have continued to develop had it not been stifled by state intervention. A vast increase in private education could be stimulated, it is suggested, if families were provided with vouchers equivalent to some notional basic educational entitlement, which families could supplement if they wished and were able to purchase education of a superior kind.

It is not proposed in the present context to say a great deal about the so-called minimal state (Nozick, 1974, pp. 149–78) whose functions are generally limited to the protection of property, defence and the maintenance of 'law and order'. Welfare provision in education and other fields is explicitly excluded from the functions of the minimal state and I have attempted to criticise the moral basis of this theory elsewhere (Wringe, 1981, pp. 74–83). Suffice it to say that democrats do not seem to be committed to either increasing or decreasing state activity. In particular circumstances they are committed only to supporting whatever arrangements most contribute to increasing the individual's control over his own life and equalising power where interests conflict in undertakings of common concern.

No great gain in freedom is made, however, if the limitations of state provision and control are replaced by subjection to market forces. These may leave many people more powerless and devoid of real choice than the imposed rules of any tyranny. Market forces are notoriously liable to favour inequalities of power and the manipulation of some people by others.

A further point must be insisted upon. Where democrats favour arrangements for state provision they are committed to the view that as far as possible these arrangements must remain subject to democratic review and control, especially by those most affected by them. In the absolutely worst case it may turn out that, as a result of human shortcomings, the arrangements of provision may become an instrument of oppression. But even in such a case the oppressor is bound to remain within the limits of what can be presented as democratic and morally justifiable. Market forces, by contrast, are subject to no such constraint unless those who *de facto* control the situation so decide.

Oppression is not solely the prerogative of governments, nor is misrepresentation. It is not obvious that knowledge is any less liable to manipulation in schools run by private entrepreneurs than in those provided by the state.

Possibly, however, the more serious objection to a massive voucher-led expansion of private education is that it would bring most benefit to those who are in a relatively fortunate position already and seems likely to work against the interests of the educationally least favoured members of our society. Unless severely means-tested, or unless the value of a basic free education is set very low, the issue of vouchers would represent a sizeable subsidy to a relatively affluent section of the community, who at present regard school fees as an obligation to be met from their own pockets.

At the other end of the scale it would seem calculated to have disastrous effects on the education of those children whose parents were unable to afford payments above the voucher rate. At present the education of these children is often overseen by education committees politically committed to advancing their interests and carried out by teachers dedicated to the same cause. It seems unlikely that educational standards would be maintained where schools were run by individuals or companies competing to extract maximum profit while offering parents something that would pass for education at about the voucher price. In particular, it is hard to see how, without incurring the charge of paternalism, governments could protect the interests of children whose parents were most likely to be taken in by educational charlatans.

It is not obvious that 'consumer choice' provides this protection. Education is in many important respects different from such commodities as washing powder or breakfast cereals. Its qualities and effects are more important, more lasting and less obvious to the non-expert. Unlike the dissatisfied supermarket shopper, the parent who has reason to be dissatisfied with his child's education may not be aware of the fact in time to 'shop elsewhere' in future.

Furthermore, though it has certainly proved possible to cut the quality of state education under the present system, it would be much easier for a government to reduce the financial value of an educational voucher, or allow it to fall behind the rate of inflation. This might be no more than an annual budgeting operation like setting income tax allowances or child benefit levels. Educational vouchers must, after all, be seen as a kind of welfare provision which adherents of the doctrine of the minimal state must wish to see reduced, perhaps until they disappear altogether. Good reasons for such a step could always be found. Financial responsibility, the need to reduce inflation or leave more cash available for investment in productive industry, the desirability of improving the lot of the elderly, and so on, are but a few of these.

It is highly predictable that under a government disposed to introduce such a scheme in the first place, the value of the voucher, and therefore the value of the education the least well off parents could afford to buy with it, would be forced steadily downwards. This is particularly likely to happen in a society in which the most influential parents would be only partially dependent on the voucher for the purchase of their own children's education and could regard it as a dispensable bonus.

It cannot convincingly be argued that the interests of the least well off could be protected by stipulating that the value of the voucher must be adequate to purchase an 'acceptable minimum' quality of education. What counts as an acceptable minimum in any field of provision is highly flexible and depends on one's point of view. This brings us once again to the anxiety that a democrat must always feel in the presence of any scheme of mixed-quality or private provision. However much he may be attracted to the 'freedom to be unequal', it is difficult for him to escape the view that a just consensus on what constitutes an acceptable minimum is only likely to be reached when 'Good enough for others' also has to mean 'Good enough for me'.

## Democracy and Diversity

Despite his rejection of mixed-quality education and his reservations about the social effects of at least some brands of private education, the democrat still has to face up to the fact of human diversity.

For whatever reason, people do seem to have, or develop, different aptitudes, different tastes, different interests, different aspirations and different temperaments. It is not self-evident that such differences would disappear if due allowance were made for class background and other aspects of previous experience. Despite popular stereotypes, it is not observed that all working-class men or all aristocratic girls have the same tastes, aptitudes and temperaments. It may even be that human beings exhibit greater differences in these respects within classes than between them.

There may also appear to be genuinely open choices of life-style and aspiration available to individuals. It is not being suggested that anyone chooses a life of poverty, deprivation and unemployment. Someone who ends up with that sort of life probably has no choice. But someone might reasonably be thought to choose between, say, a life of tranquillity and relative comfort, a life of action and ambition, or a life of dedication to some ideal such as the pursuit of truth or artistic performance, even though he does not consciously make such a choice at a particular moment.

A supporter of liberal democracy might say that each of these modes of life was equally valid and that the right choice for an individual would be as much a matter of taste and temperament as anything else. It is also possible to think of there being genuine choices of the occupation in which one realises these various styles of life. One does not have to invoke social determinism to account for someone's choice of the contented life of a skilled craftsman or the quiet dedication of a country curate, rather than the hurly-burly existence of a thrusting businessman or trade union official.

If at least some of these choices are genuinely valid ones, it cannot be that the democrat is committed to preventing people from choosing diversely in the name of equality. The democrat is not committed to suppressing differences of life-style or occupation as such. He is simply committed to ensuring that, as far as possible, people do have the genuine opportunity to choose their life-style, and that no one is forced to 'choose' a life of drudgery, physical exhaustion and insecurity because he has no realistic alternative. He is, however, also committed to ensuring that as far as possible the possessors of all tastes, talents and temperaments, the adherents of all varieties of life-style and the members of all occupations have equal opportunities to control their own lives and exercise equal influence on common undertakings.

In one thing at least Mill and the supporters of private education are right. Even if private education is not necessary to bring it about, the world is a better place for many people if a variety of life-styles, occupations and activities are available to choose from, for this increases the likelihood that any one individual will achieve satisfaction. This argument only works, however, if individuals actually are free and able to choose, and do not fall into one life-style or occupation through ignorance or get pushed into another for the sake of prestige or as a consequence of their social origins.

The problem for the democrat is that differences of taste, temperament and aptitude, of previous learning as well as of aspiration and future occupation, seem to require curricular diversity. To suggest that all children, whatever their aptitudes, tastes, temperaments, previous learnings, and so on, ought to achieve the same educational outcomes is, in the present state of our pedagogic skills, a recipe for creating failures. It is difficult to see how a democrat can favour this, for this is to legitimate subordination and in many cases to inflict a hurt that is undeserved.

Curricular diversity, however, also presents the democrat with problems. Pupils who follow certain curricula – those stressing the symbolic skills of language, mathematics and science – have more options open to them than others.

But even democrats are not committed to performing the impossible, and this means impossible in the present state of our pedagogic skills. With the best will in the world we do not seem to have found ways of enabling all children to get very far in some subjects. In particular we have not found ways of motivating all pupils to apply themselves to work at the symbolic skills that would enable them to change their lives.

So is the democrat to give up and accept that different curricula are appropriate to different children? Is he bound to further concede that for the sake of efficiency different 'kinds' of children should not only be taught different things, but should also be taught by different teachers in different rooms or even different buildings? Does he further have to admit that the earlier different 'kinds' of children are identified the better, so that no one spends more time than necessary following an unsuitable curriculum? (Note that I am not here talking about Cooper's mixed-quality education. The possibility that less care, attention and resources should be devoted to the education of those who do not learn academic subjects so easily is not here even under consideration. All of the above possibilities are quite compatible with devoting as much or more effort and resources to the teaching of those who find the going tougher.)

To settle for separate and entirely different educational experiences for those of differing aptitudes, inclinations and temperaments is to concede too much. Despite differences that may exist between them, there are many things all children need to learn. In a modern democracy this includes learning to get on with people with different tastes, attitudes and understandings from oneself. But there are also more academic things all children need to know. Attempts have been made (DES/HMI, 1977, 1980; DES/WO, 1977, 1979, 1980, 1981) to define a core of common learnings that all children should have the chance to achieve. John White (1973) argues that all children should receive some initiation into all the so-called forms of knowledge. In later chapters (see below, pp. 89–90) I shall consider the view that in a democracy all citizens need to have some understanding of these if the democratic form of government is to function properly.

There are a number of special reasons why a committed democrat should favour common learning experiences for as long as is practicable. First, if all are to have their chance of influencing and managing things that concern them, democracy has to be characterised by fluidity and the possibility of individuals interchanging roles. Despite the fact that some writers of even such apparent democratic commitment as Mannheim (1950, pp. 87–107) may be discovered urging the importance of 'elites' and their education, it is difficult to see how one can reconcile such a commitment with the idea of a separate education from an early stage of those who are to rule and those who are to obey.

Secondly, democracy has to operate through discussion and willing co-operation. This is not a question of being able to 'handle' the other person as conceived of in manuals of man management, but of under-standing and attempting to accommodate his point of view, respecting the values he regards as important, and seeing his reasons as genuine reasons and not merely as obstacles to one's own will or to what one sees from one's own point of view as the common good.

There is a third point, closely connected with the above. Given that everyone is entitled to regard his own purposes as important, a good democratic solution to a problem is not one that over-rules the other's point of view by means of a majority vote, nor a mere compromise that results in no one's getting more than half of what he wants. Ideally, it is one that promotes both (or all) interests, and such a solution is most likely to be found when those involved in the discussion each understand more of what the other wants than the other has yet put into words.

Now it may be that claims for mixed ability teaching, common curricula and common schools have been greatly exaggerated. In the same classroom, listening to the same formal class lesson, different pupils may learn quite different things. In co-operative groupwork different learnings may result from the different roles pupils play in the group as the result of differences of temperament, ability, experience, and so on.

Nevertheless, it is at least a reasonable presumption that the understandings and abilities listed above as being appropriate to a democracy are not likely to be helped by the physical separation of different groups of children into different classrooms or different schools studying different subjects with different teachers having different values and different educational priorities. Account may also need to be taken of the thoroughly human temptation to promote internal cohesion by encouraging external hostility towards pupils, teachers and practices 'at the other place'. What applies to the physical separation of schools applies to a lesser extent to the physical separation of different ability groups within the same building.

This would all seem to suggest that democrats ought to be in favour of developments in the direction of shared curricula, common schools, mixed ability classrooms, and so on. To favour developments that will make these things practical, however, is not the same as being committed to their immediate implementation as of now, come what may. It is difficult to see how any reasonable person can be committed to, say, mixed ability teaching that results in a shambles in which no one learns anything, and teachers find their working lives intolerable. Nor can such a person feel that his commitments are so important that he is entitled to impose them on others who are not persuaded of their value. The most he can be committed to is working for a situation and a development of educational skills that will eventually make these things possible.

We need also to be clear, however, that what is possible is not the same as what is consistent with maximum academic efficiency, far less with the maximum academic achievement of the ablest. There is more to education than purely academic achievement, and the learnings necessary to function appropriately in a democracy are part of this. In defending comprehensive schools, the maximisation of common learning experiences and mixed ability classes, it is not necessary to take on board the claim that these are also the most academically efficient teaching arrangements. The person who makes maximum academic achievement, and more especially the maximum academic achievement of the ablest, the *sine qua non* of an acceptable educational institution has other commitments than those of the democrat.

It is not here being argued that the ablest are to be held back 'for the sake of equality'. No gratuitous levelling down is being suggested. It is simply that in an imperfect world the ablest also have their part to play in the general round of compromises that are necessary in order that all may have the chance of seeing some of their aspirations fulfilled.

# 6

# The Democratic Government of Education

## Introduction

To be committed to democracy is to be committed to a certain view of the power relations in which individuals and institutions should stand to each other in society. To say, however, that education should be 'more democratic' or 'as democratic as possible' is notoriously ambiguous. Such slogans may be used to support demands for almost every imaginable distribution of power in the educational world. At one extreme, democracy has been urged as a reason for giving pupils more say in the content of their education and the running of their schools. At the other, it may be used as an argument for making schools more 'accountable' to the government and thereby to voters and taxpayers, that is, as an argument for greater centralisation and control.

In Chapter 3 it was argued that there is no contradiction between being committed to democracy and conceding that the internal organisation of some institutions might be relatively hierarchical if that were most likely to produce results of which all, including those in the institution, would be likely to approve. It may therefore reasonably be asked whether schools are likely to achieve such desirable results under the authoritarian command of an autocratic head. That they are likely to do so is no doubt the view of those who speak of 'decisive leadership' and 'effective' headteachers, or compare the headteacher to the captain of a ship, the general in command of an army, or the managing director of an industrial firm.

These comparisons, however, are not entirely valid. There are important differences between the work of ships, armies and firms on the one hand and that of educational institutions on the other. There is usually little disagreement as to the destination of ships, or the purposes of armies or firms. The person in charge is simply required to provide the necessary know-how and inspiration. Nor is there often much argument about the criteria according to which the success of ships, armies, or firms is to be judged. Experience, possibly backed up by certain technical knowledge, will probably indicate the most likely means of achieving ends which are regarded as desirable by all.

Educational institutions are organisations of a different kind. The most important disagreements in education are not usually about the best means of achieving agreed ends at all. Almost without exception the questions that divide teachers and educationists are about what are the most desirable ends. This is often so even when the issue is expressed in empirical terms of which teaching methods or organisational arrangements produce the best results when the results to be obtained are fairly closely specified and appear to be agreed by both sides.

Two examples may suffice to illustrate this point. The argument about whether or not comprehensive systems produce better academic results than selective (i.e. grammar and secondary modern) schools, and the question of whether traditional or child-centred teaching styles are more effective in producing pupils' progress at primary level, are ostensibly empirical questions. It ought to be possible to settle them by empirical investigation.

The fact that they have not been so settled suggests that the facts and figures produced in investigations of these questions are little more than ammunition in a much more fundamental controversy between those who are already committed to comprehensive schools or child-centred education and those who, for whatever reason, are committed to their opposites. Teachers and students who read this book will be well aware that the various disputes about teaching methods in their subjects are more often about what is to count as competence in French, science, maths, or whatever, than about the most efficient means of achieving results which all agree to be desirable.

Matters of policy in a school concern such things as the school's aims and ethos. Whether a school streams and sets at the earliest possible moment or whether it continues with mixed ability classes for as long as it can, will probably depend on someone's view of the relative importance of high academic achievement by the ablest pupils and not creating 'sink' classes of 'low expectation' children taught by low expectation teachers. Whether the timetable is made out in terms of traditional academic subjects taught by the members of traditionally named departments or whether there is a substantial measure of curriculum integration will also reflect someone's view of what constitutes a proper education.

Priorities and choices of this kind are not a matter of technical expertise, but questions of value upon which there can be no ultimate authority. Faced with the need for judgements of this kind in determining the educational policies of schools and teachers, it is possible to adopt two quite different strategies. Either one appoints someone to 'lay down the law' on policy matters and delegate clearly delineated areas of responsibility to others. Or one may attempt to build in arrangements for allowing all who will be affected by and have a legitimate interest in what happens in the school to 'have their say' and exercise their due portion of influence over what is to take place.

Until recently the first of the two above-mentioned strategies was almost universally regarded as the correct one. Once appointed, the head of a maintained school was supposed to assume more or less sole responsibility for the entire curriculum, management and organisation of the school. The only legal constraint to which he was subject was to ensure that each day began with a communal act of worship and that children whose parents did not object received a period of religious education each week. It is true that local education authorities were charged with a general responsibility for the curriculum but in practice this was delegated to headteachers, and to no one else.

Such an arrangement was possible since there was, for a long time, a considerable degree of consensus both about how schools should be run and about what should be taught to various categories of children. Heads, though apparently in a position to be autocratic, rarely found themselves in fundamental conflict either with prevailing professional opinion, as represented by university examination boards, for example, or with the views of responsible citizens who composed their local authorities and boards of governors. Educational issues and ideals did not divide the major political parties, and assistant teachers, not to mention parents and children, all knew their places.

Needless to say, recent years have seen substantial changes in both attitudes and practice. Educationists and politicians have perceived that today's pupils are tomorrow's citizens, and that the nature of their educational experience will profoundly affect, even if it does not actually determine, the form of tomorrow's society. Ideological differences now divide not only teachers but also parents and pupils.

The emergence of various rights agitations, both connected and unconnected with education, has emphasised the importance to the dignity of the individual of having one's say and being consulted, rather than accepting existing practice and traditional authority.

When consensus no longer exists, autocracy is no longer tolerable and needs to be replaced by mechanisms which are capable either of restoring consensus or, failing that, of providing decision procedures that are visibly just. Recurring economic crises and anxieties about educational standards, allied perhaps with a genuine concern for greater openness in public institutions, have also given rise to a degree of overt central guidance to schools in curricular matters and a call for greater public accountability on the part of teachers and schools.

Since, as was observed, almost any demand for a redistribution of power between headteachers, the political authorities, staff, parents and children can be couched in terms of 'more democracy', it is proposed, in the following pages, to consider the democratic credentials of arguments for greater public accountability, a greater degree of staff involvement in the management of schools, and greater degrees of parent power and pupil power.

## Public Accountability

No doubt between the 1920s and the late 1960s many headteachers informally consulted their staff and governors about the curriculum of their schools. But they did not always do so, and were not felt to be under any obligation in this respect. The 1960s, however, saw a rapid development in the advisory services of local educational authorities, and advisers were often able to exert considerable influence on curricular development, both in particular subjects and in schools as a whole. This was often made easier by their power to allocate additional funds for resources and equipment. More spectacularly, from 1977 onwards there has issued from both the Department of Education and Science and Her Majesty's Inspectorate a stream of discussion papers, reports and surveys aimed at influencing the nature of the curriculum (DES/HMI, 1977, 1980; DES/WO, 1977, 1979, 1980, 1981).

In addition, the Manpower Services Commission is now in a position to influence the education and training of many 16–18 year olds, and some 14–16 year olds, through the allocation of funds for training programmes. The setting up in 1976 of an Assessment of Performance Unit to devise procedures and establish criteria to assess the performance of the educational system as a whole has also helped to establish the notion of the schools' accountability to the public.

It ought perhaps to be stressed that none of the documents coming from official sources is presented as being in any way mandatory upon local authorities, schools, or teachers. Nevertheless, the publication of opinions, recommendations, surveys of 'the national picture' or descriptions of 'good practice' coupled with the power to inspect, assess and report must be regarded as a considered attempt to coerce. This is particularly true in a situation of teacher unemployment, institutional change and professional insecurity. These developments have aroused considerable discussion. At a philosophical level (see, for example,

Sockett, 1980) this has focused on the issues of academic freedom and teacher accountability.

On the one hand, it may be argued that since education is provided at public expense, the public is at least entitled to discover in what ways and how successfully its resources are being used. The public provision of education may also seem to justify some degree of public control over what is taught.

Against this it is possible to invoke the spectre of political indoctrination and state-approved knowledge. This is of particular importance in a democracy, in so far as the way people vote may depend on the values they have acquired at school, and on their knowledge or ignorance of the way public affairs are carried on. In this respect, it may be claimed that a democratic public has an over-riding interest in maintaining the integrity and independence of a teaching profession dedicated as a matter of first priority to the teaching of truth and to the development in its pupils of critical standards appropriate to various forms of knowledge and evaluation. Arguably, such independence may be jeopardised if teachers' objectives are specified too closely or if their fortunes are too closely linked with observed performance.

## Teacher Participation in School Policy Decisions

Readers will doubtless be aware that despite pressure for centralisation and public accountability the headteacher in most schools is unequivocally in charge. According to the so-called Model Articles of Government and Rules of Management drawn up under the 1944 Education Act, he is legally responsible for the conduct, curriculum, internal organisation, management and discipline of the school. He will normally have the power to recommend the approval of a new teacher's probation. He can promote teachers within the school and writes reports on teachers applying for promotion elsewhere. He also allocates funds and resources, decides the timetable of individual teachers and determines the place an individual's or a department's subject will occupy in the curriculum. At the present time he may also have the power of recommending particular teachers for redundancy or redeployment.

Of course, many headteachers, especially in larger schools, will delegate many of their responsibilities to their managerial team of deputies and senior teachers, as well as to year heads, heads of faculty, heads of department, and so on. Many too will use 'consultation' as a managerial strategy, to find out which of their policies will be welcomed and which will need to be imposed. There are also, no doubt, heads who see genuine consultation as right and proper given that different people

69

have different points of view and different but equally valid educational priorities.

Since, however, heads actually have the power to coerce, they may ultimately be held responsible for whatever is done in their schools. Most of them feel in consequence that they cannot delegate ultimate power in any matter. The majority vote of a staff committee or even of a full staff meeting would simply not be accepted as a reason for adopting one policy rather than another by many people outside the school – or for that matter by some people inside the school who disagreed with whatever decision was taken.

Considerations of this kind have led the National Union of Teachers, many of whose members and officers are themselves heads, to propose (NUT, 1971) that responsibility for certain important policy matters should be lifted from headteachers and become the legal responsibility either of the staff as a whole or of a representative staff council. The policy matters in relation to which this proposal is made are: the curriculum, school organisation, internal school finance and parent-teacher relations.

If this were done, it is proposed (p. 6) that heads should retain executive responsibility for the day-to-day running of the school and be responsible to the staff or staff council for carrying out collectively decided policies. As the NUT document points out, there is no inherent absurdity in such an arrangement, which closely resembles the situation in many colleges and universities where the academic board or senate may be ultimately responsible for many areas of policy.

The document gives a number of arguments in favour of a greater degree of teacher participation in school decision-making. These include changes in educational practice which require a great deal of collective and co-operative effort from colleagues, the greater complexity and size of schools, so that no one individual can be expected to have a totally rounded and balanced view of the whole, and a general tendency both in educational institutions and in society generally for individuals to demand a greater say in matters that concern them.

But possibly the most significant reason the document gives is that 'the speed of change within the educational system is such that of itself it creates a demand for a say in the way things are developing' (p. 4). In a static situation individuals may be prepared to rub along with things as they are. But when everything is up for grabs people need both information and a chance to state their point of view. Otherwise things they care deeply about, whole areas of valued activity, not to mention their actual job, may be organised out of existence before they know it.

More radical than the NUT study outline is the pamphlet *Democracy in Schools* produced by Rank and File, a splinter group within the

NUT. This group proposed to reform not only the authority structure within the school but also the constitution of governing and managing bodies. According to *Democracy in Schools* these bodies should consist of equal numbers of LEA representatives and representatives of parents' council, a staff council and a school council (elected by pupils).

The claims of parents and pupils to participation in the management of schools will be considered separately. For the present it is to be noted that the document proposes that the staff council be given most of the powers and responsibilities currently resting with heads, as well as the responsibility 'periodically to elect from its members an Executive Officer . . . and a deputy . . . in consultation with the Governing Body' (p. 12). The executive officer is, of course, intended to replace the traditional head. He or she would be accountable to the staff council and would be replaceable by it.

If it is thought that Rank and File is a somewhat extreme and irresponsible group it should be noted that the Taylor Committee, a committee of inquiry appointed by the then Minister of State for Education and Science and the Secretary of State for Wales, also recommends a new kind of governing body for schools which 'should consist of equal numbers of LEA representatives, school staff, parents (with, where appropriate, pupils) and representatives of the local community' (DES/WO, 1977, p. 111). Current arrangements whereby the governing bodies of schools include a small number of elected staff and parent representatives may be regarded as steps towards the implementation of this committee's recommendations.

In recent years philosophers, politicians and a government committee of inquiry (DT, 1977; Smith, 1977; P. White, 1979) have given thought to proposals for industrial or workplace democracy. Arguments in favour of such proposals generally may often be enlisted in support of teachers' claims to have a substantial say in the management of their schools. Such arguments may be based on the claim of the individual as a moral agent to control his own activities, or they may be based on the view that the aims of an institution are likely to be better achieved if the institution is democratically or collectively governed by its members.

Prominent among the first group of arguments is the consideration that the moral agent cannot ultimately divest himself of his freedom and responsibility to act as he thinks right without ceasing to be a moral agent (P. White, 1979). As we saw in Chapter 3, this does not mean that a moral agent can never accept instructions from others, for this may be necessary for the accomplishment of common purposes from which all benefit and of which all may approve. It does suggest, however, that democratic workplace procedures ought to be introduced, at least up to the point where they are found to be positively counter-productive.

71

It may with some plausibility be argued, however, that far from being inefficient, participation may have positively beneficial effects on the achievement of an organisation's aims. Those who oppose employee participation often have a conflictual view of industrial relations according to which giving more power to workers simply obstructs the work of management and is bound to lead to a less efficient organisation. This view may rest on two assumptions. The first of these is that all knowledge comes from 'the top'. The other is that only management really has the goals of the institution at heart and that power or influence given to subordinate employees will simply be used for extracting more money or easier working conditions.

A more modern view of industrial relations stresses that both management and other employees have a common interest in their organisation's performance. If the situation is seen in this light it will seem more natural to seek co-operation rather than confrontation. It has long been known that many people perform better when valued, taken notice of and made to feel 'involved'. But there are a number of further reasons why management should listen to those they manage.

Often some relatively minor grouse which can be easily attended to may be demoralising and a cause of resentment. Workers may also be well placed to make valuable suggestions which will improve efficiency. The management that takes the view that anything subordinates have to say must necessarily be based on antagonism or ignorance cuts itself off from a source of both goodwill and good ideas. This fact is nowadays widely recognised and both formal and informal arrangements for employee consultation exist in many organisations.

What is perhaps less widely recognised is that to use consultation simply as a tool of management, as a means of getting more commitment and therefore more and better work out of one's subordinates while actually denying them any real power in matters of importance, is fundamentally dishonest and may be rejected once it is recognised for what it is. This suggests that ultimately participation cannot stop short of some degree of actual control. In industry this may inspire demands for substantial representation at boardroom level. Such is not only the policy of the TUC in Britain but a legal requirement in many European countries.

Arguments justifying employee participation in the management of industrial concerns would seem to apply with even more force in the case of teachers seeking to participate in the management of their schools. In a democracy it must be assumed that all citizens are capable of some degree of rational, prudent and moral judgement and action. Those who become teachers have received a more extended and more thorough education and have probably derived more benefit from it than many other people. For the most recent part of their education they will have worked fairly independently and have exercised a good deal of freedom and responsibility for the organisation and quality of their own work. They are also expected to be committed to certain educational aims, whether the main emphasis in these is placed on the propagation of their subject or the good of their pupils.

In the past the professional responsibility of teachers was expressed in the recognition that what they did in their own classrooms was very much their own affair. The greater degree of planning, co-operation and co-ordination necessary in today's schools means that the individual teacher has less freedom inside the classroom than he used to have. Among rational individuals committed to educational aims which may be different but equally valid, the appropriate model of co-ordination is provided not by standardisation and control from above but by discussion and compromise. If complete consensus is not possible then at least mutual accommodation may be aimed at. The motivational benefits of being given one's head and treated as a responsible person are likely to prove at least as great among teachers as among industrial workers, as are the benefits of allowing information and ideas to flow 'upwards' as well as in the contrary direction. Indeed, one well-known headmaster, who is an advocate of teacher participation, stresses the importance of young teachers entering the profession as a source of ideas and enthusiasm necessary to keep the process of educational change in motion (Watts, 1977, pp. 123–31).

An authoritarian view of education sees teachers as carrying out the instructions of heads transmitted via heads of department and processing pupils to make them into acceptable 'products' by the time they leave school. An alternative view might regard them as identifying and attending to their pupils' educational needs in a responsible, self-regulating way, negotiating with and where necessary putting pressure on school authorities to provide materials and other conditions required for this end. Both of these are conflictual and rather extreme views. No doubt it is preferable to see both teachers and administrators as engaged in co-operation for the achievement of a plurality of educational goals.

## Parent Participation in the Management of Schools

In Chapter 4 we saw that the defenders of private schooling may point to the paragraph in the *United Nations Universal Declaration of Human Rights*, Article 26 (iii), which insists that 'Parents have a prior right to choose the kind of education that shall be given to their children'. If this is indeed a right, it would seem to be a right of all parents, not just of those that can afford to educate their children privately.

It is, of course, true that in a parliamentary democracy such as our own parents may, in a very indirect sense, be said to choose the education their children shall receive, in so far as they vote for parties offering different educational programmes. But a vote in periodic elections in which educational policy is but one item in an electoral package is a blunt instrument with which to control things that are important to us. In the education of our children, as in many other important matters, there is no reason why individuals' power to influence the conditions of their lives should stop there.

It is not entirely clear what moral entitlements arise from parenthood (O'Neill and Ruddick, 1979; Aiken and Lafollette, 1980). Children do not 'belong' to parents in quite the way items of property belong to them. People other than parents may be thought to have a legitimate interest in how children are educated. The state or community, for example, may be thought to have a legitimate interest in ensuring that children grow up relatively law-abiding, or at least not entirely anti-social. It may also be thought that the state has a duty to intervene to protect the interests of children when parents fail to ensure that they are educated adequately.

Nevertheless, it is difficult to deny the right of parents to exercise some direct influence over what goes on in the schools to which they are obliged to send their children. This would seem to be particularly clear in the case of parents who have no effective choice in their children's schools.

Objection may be made to so-called interference by parents in the professional work of schools, and some genuine misgivings may be felt regarding parent governors. Teachers might feel threatened in their authority if a rebuked third-former could say 'Look, my father's one of your governors, so watch it'. It might also be argued that parents, not being experts, are in no position to express views about what takes place in schools, far less participate in their management. It is sometimes suggested, too, that parent governors will be primarily concerned to advance the interests of their own children rather than the good of the school as a whole.

None of these objections is entirely persuasive, and some of them are objections to democracy in general rather than particular to educational democracy. The Taylor Report's proposal (DES/WO, 1977, p. 111) is for one-third parent governors, who would always be outnumbered by staff and LEA representatives. The supposed undermining of the teacher's authority is not to be taken too seriously. The teacher who relies on being able to inflict unpleasantness without fear of come-back has little justification in asking to be protected by the system. Besides, one of the advantages of democratising the management of schools is precisely that it avoids the kind of situation in which teachers are unrepresented and need to go in fear and trembling lest some ill-informed and all-powerful governor should take against them.

The objection that parents have little expert knowledge in the field of education is not strong either. As we saw earlier, arguments from expertise are not always conclusive in educational matters. It is frequently the case in democracies that experts are required to explain and justify themselves to non-experts. If the latter have less expert knowledge than the professionals, they may have the advantage of detachment and balanced judgement in assessing the latest professional bandwagon or enthusiasm. Though not often professionally knowledgeable, parents have the advantage of being closely in touch with their children, and in a position to see aspects of their out-of-school lives and their response to their school experience which are hidden from headteachers and their staff. The objection is in any case invalid if it is intended as a defence of the present position. Many governors at the moment have neither professional expertise nor any particularly close acquaintance with children.

Normally parents may be presumed to be committed to the good of their children, even though we may think their conception of this good is misguided. The same does not necessarily apply to all existing governors who may include local businessmen, clergymen of one denomination or another, ratepayers' representatives, or political nominees who, however great their integrity, will necessarily have other loyalties to consider.

Parent governors will, of course, be conscious of the interests of their own children. That representatives are inclined to look to their own sectional interests and the interests of those close to them is a defect inherent in representative democracy and must be accepted along with it. But no child can possibly have more than two parents on a board of governors, and these will always be a minority. The too blatant advocacy of policies favourable to one's own children is liable to be resented, and is unlikely to command support.

The danger of a highly politicised faction on a governing body is a real one as it is in democratic politics generally. Such a group would, however, be constrained not only by the presence of other representative groups, but also by the framework of law and regulations by which the conduct of education is governed. A group of National Front or hysterically left-wing parent governors might prove disagreeable but it is hard to see how they could turn the school into an instrument of overt political indoctrination or racial persecution. The danger presented by such a group is far less than that presented by a politically or racially prejudiced head and no greater than that presented by prejudiced governors in the existing scheme of things.

Thus it would seem that most of the more commonly heard objections to substantial parent representation on school governing bodies are less than conclusive. In addition to the claim that parents have a right to influence the conditions under which their children are educated, considerable weight must also be given to the other category of arguments normally put forward in favour of greater participation and involvement – namely, that benefits are likely to spring from such an arrangement.

The school in which there is contact, communication and trust between parents and teachers would seem bound to be better than one in which the relationship is one of mutual suspicion and hostility. The more parents are involved in their children's education, the more likely it would seem that this education will be successful. The experience of participatory democracy itself may also be educative. Parents may not be experts in educational matters. But discussion with those who are experts is likely to enhance rather than diminish such understanding as they have. It cannot be bad that at least some parents should gain a greater understanding of the world in which their children spend the greater part of their day.

## Democracy and Pupil Power

During the interwar years a number of progressive and dedicated individuals experimented with the idea of running schools as democratic communities of various kinds (see Neill, 1962, 1973; Skidelsky, 1969; Berg, 1971). To attempt to run schools in this way was held both to be desirable in itself and to have certain beneficial effects on pupils' personal, psychological and moral development. In particular it was thought to have beneficial effects on recalcitrant young people whose delinquency was supposed to be caused by the authoritarian institutions in which they had been educated previously.

More recently, in the late 1960s and early 1970s, rather more vociferous demands were made, both by young people themselves and by others on their behalf, for so-called pupils' rights (Wringe, 1981, pp.5–20). Many of these demands were for rights of freedom in such matters as personal appearance, the use of alcohol, tobacco and other drugs, and sexual association. Demands were, however, also made for the right of pupils to participate in the management of their schools. This movement is no longer strong, but there remain some schools which continue to have token pupil representatives at governors' and other meetings, as well as a rather larger number of schools with school councils that continue to discuss a limited range of school matters.

Arguments in favour of 'pupil participation' again fall into two by now familiar categories: those that claim educational benefits for it, and those which claim that school pupils, just like anyone else, have a right to some say in matters that closely concern them.

The view that pupils' participation in the management of their schools has an important part to play in the education – especially the political education – of children will be examined in more detail later. In the present chapter it is proposed simply to set out and comment on various arguments to the effect that to be committed to democracy is to be committed to the view that children have the right to a say in the management of their schools, irrespective of any contribution this may make to the educational goals of their teachers.

It will be recalled that a central justification of democracy was that the individual has purposes that are as important to him as the purposes of others are to them. It is also to be assumed that the individual is normally most likely to achieve these purposes if he is allowed to choose the means to those ends himself, subject to similar rights in others.

The problem in the case of children is that since they are in a state of fairly rapid development, purposes that seem important to them now may seem less so in the not too distant future. Also, given their limited experience and, perhaps, limited reasoning powers they not only risk choosing trivial or otherwise misguided ends for themselves, but may also be hopelessly injudicious in their choice of means.

Children may therefore be thought not to have an interest in having too much freedom. Indeed, it may be thought that while they are young they have a right to have certain choices made for them and to receive the guidance, support and indeed the coercion necessary to ensure that they do what is necessary to achieve the ends they would choose for themselves if they were fully rational.

Where rights of participation are concerned, there is a further complication. To participate in the control of joint enterprises is to choose ends and means not only for oneself but also for others. All democrats must accept that other fully rational beings may have the same degree of influence in affairs as they have themselves, and that their own preferred course of action may sometimes be over-ruled. It would, however, seem much less reasonable to expect mature, knowledgeable and rational adults to see their various purposes frustrated by the votes of children, if it is accepted that these are not yet fully rational and are particularly likely to be swayed by demagoguery, momentary enthusiasm, or mere whim.

In the case of pupils and teachers there is yet another twist to the story. By definition, it is argued (Olafson, 1973), the relationship between teachers and pupils is an unequal or 'asymmetrical' one. To be a pupil, the argument goes, is precisely to be one who does not fully grasp the nature of the educational goals and standards that are being set before one. Individually and collectively, therefore, pupils are in no position to choose these goals and standards for themselves, nor are they in any position to choose the means and processes by which they are to be achieved, or to judge the competence of those who teach them.

The school is not a sovereign state answerable to no one but itself but an institution within a wider institutional framework. It is provided by the adult community for fairly specific purposes. Decisions regarding much that goes on in schools must therefore quite properly be regarded as *ultra vires* to any committee or assembly of school members, whether children or adults. This is not necessarily undemocratic. All deliberating bodies in a democracy have their terms of reference.

Unfortunately, however, the outside community rather than the school must largely determine the relations of authority and obedience that exist between teachers and pupils. The adult members of schools are quite properly held responsible by the community at large for what happens to the children in them. This may be regarded as a reasonable condition on which parents hand over their children to the educational authority. Yet teachers can scarcely be held responsible for the safety, good order and learning of children in schools if they have not the authority to give necessary instructions and apply whatever sanctions are necessary to ensure they are carried out.

It is sometimes said that there are areas of school life which may be safely given over to pupil management since they do not concern such weighty matters as safety, educational policy, or the distribution of substantial resources. If this seems to offer an attractive compromise to the democratically minded educator it must be pointed out that pupil radicals and their adult supporters have long ago warned of the dangers of accepting lap-dog school councils which discuss trivial matters but have no real powers.

Councils whose agenda is decided by the head and who spend their time discussing 'How we can improve the standard of morning assembly' or 'What should be done about the problem of litter', and in which the headteacher's veto is written into the constitution and regularly invoked, are bound to be regarded with contempt.

There appears to be no obvious way out of the dilemma posed by developing persons in a democracy. On the one hand we have the prospect of an unacceptable and unmanageable degree of pupil power which cannot be rendered responsible. On the other, we have sham school/house/year councils which may go through the formal procedures of democracy (speaking through the chair, proposing and seconding motions, voting) without either power or responsibility, and therefore lack the very essence of democracy. Yet it is difficult to see how the case for some degree of genuine pupil participation can be denied. Young people are allowed to marry at 16 and to vote in parliamentary and local elections as well as making binding legal contracts at 18. It is therefore difficult to see how they can be regarded as totally lacking powers of rational deliberation as they approach those ages.

Measures of partial democratisation are likely to please no one, being regarded as hopelessly naïve and impractical by the conservative, while the radical see them as unexciting, not to say fraudulent, attempts to give the impression of enlightenment without conceding anything of substance. Despite this final objection, however, the only way forward would seem to be via some partial and discretionary form of pupil participation, for only thus can the experience of collective self-management be gained under conditions that do not court disaster and disillusionment.

It is not an uncommon experience in liberal democracies for progressive measures to be rejected by both left and right. The only response that a liberal democrat can make to this is to continue earnestly explaining the reasons for the extent and limitation of his proposals on the presumption that even some of those who hold extreme views may do so in good faith and eventually be open to persuasion and the evidence of experience – or produce arguments which he himself will see as adequate grounds for changing his own views.

# 7

# Education and Democracy

Before exploring the question of whether any particular kind of educational content is appropriate to citizens of a democracy, we need to take note of the view that democracy is unique among possible forms of government in that there are special links between it and education. It can be argued (Wollheim, 1966, p. 266) that there is a logical requirement and the citizens of a democracy should be educated. All regimes, if they are to persist, require some means of socialising the young into the roles they are later to occupy. Despotisms, for instance, would seem likely to function more efficiently if the habits of fear and obedience are inculcated from an early age. Polities based on distinctions of class require habits of deference and respect, religious and totalitarian states depend on indoctrination into the official faith, and so on.

Beyond these things, and such skills as are necessary to stay alive and serve the interests of their masters, however, little else is required of the lower orders. Absolute monarchs and dictators may promote some form of education out of benevolence or idealism, but it is not implied in the notion of a monarch or a dictator, or whatever, that he should do so. Indeed, it is characteristic of undemocratic regimes that education of the lower orders has often been regarded as unnecessary or even subversive.

Democracies, by contrast, can only truly be so described if their citizens have some measure of education. This is almost as fundamental a requirement as the existence of some system such as voting whereby citizens express their will. For the point of voting is not marking a paper or raising the hand, but the fact that the citizen makes a choice. But it is difficult to see how citizens can be said to choose between either policies or rulers – as opposed to simply plumping for one or the other – without possessing some canons of judgement, some information and some means of assessing its reliability or relevance.

Only extreme versions of the 'alternative' theory of democracy, in which candidates for government are supposed simply to compete for votes by whatever means seem most likely to succeed, would seem compatible with an uneducated electorate. If, as may be the case, there exist states in which 'voters' have little conception either of the policies at issue or of the reasons for choosing one candidate rather than another, we may hesitate as to whether such states are properly termed democracies. The point of democracy, it will be recalled, is that it is the form of government most likely to give the individual equality of influence over joint undertakings, especially over those that most closely concern him. The 'voter' who marks his paper, or whatever, without being in a position to judge the likely outcome of how he votes cannot be said to have any kind of meaningful voice in the affairs of his community.

The absurdities of an uneducated electorate have often been stressed by the opponents of democracy and those opposed to extending the suffrage to certain classes of people such as the poor, native peoples in colonial territories and black people in the southern states of America. When poverty or race no longer served in themselves as grounds for excluding some people from the suffrage, ignorance and illiteracy were sometimes put forward as reasons for denying the vote to the same groups.

The necessity of an educated electorate is also recognised by John Stuart Mill who is widely regarded as one of the foremost proponents of the democratic ideal. Mill (1861, p. 218) gives as one of the three conditions which must be fulfilled before democracy can be regarded as a suitable form of government that a people 'should be willing and able to fulfil the duties and discharge the functions which it [democracy] imposes on them'. It is clear that for him one important element in the ability to fulfil the duties of democracy is constituted by education. Later in the same work he writes (p. 280): 'I regard it as wholly inadmissible that any person should participate in the suffrage without being able to read and write and, I will add, perform the common operations of arithmetic.'

We may disagree with Mill's particular requirements. Mere literacy may seem at once unnecessary and inadequate to enable people to participate effectively in democracy. There is, however, no reason to regard Mill's declaration that 'universal teaching must precede universal enfranchisement' as an insincere delaying tactic aimed at holding on to the privilege of voting for the educated upper and middle classes. The test of Mill's sincerity is that throughout his life he devoted himself tirelessly to the cause of universal education.

For Mill – in keeping with his philosophical views generally – the connection between education and democracy was an empirical one. He

81

simply thought that an ignorant electorate would be bound to choose unsuitable representatives and that under such circumstances democracy would collapse or revert to some less desirable and less demanding form of government. That the institutions of democracy would in fact collapse in a state in which a large part of the electorate was illiterate or more generally ignorant may seem less obvious to us than it did to Mill. In any case, this argument is to be clearly distinguished from that advanced at the beginning of this chapter. There it was held, not that democratic institutions would collapse if the electorate were ignorant, but that even if the institutional forms of democracy survived, a country in which electors did not understand what they were voting for would be no democracy.

There are further links between the concepts of education and democracy. One of the grounds which may be urged in favour of democracy – especially participatory democracy – as a form of government is that the practice of democracy is in itself an educative process. There are really two versions of this argument.

First, it is true that a large part may be played in modern election campaigns by such unedifying activities as media management, the use of pat slogans, emotive appeals, character assassination, and so on. Nevertheless, in any such campaign electors will, however unwillingly, hear and read political argument of a kind, even though we may deplore the quality of the argument and the degree of reflection with which it is received. Ultimately voters, unless we suppose that they are completely frivolous or creatures of habit, must either choose between two or more sets of policies or make a judgement as to the credibility of one candidate rather than others.

However apathetic or fixed in his views the voter may be, it would be surprising if an election campaign did not leave him with some additional knowledge of the issues involved in governing the nation, or some increased awareness of the complexity of issues he had previously regarded as simple and straightforward. We may not entirely share Mill's optimistic view (Garforth, 1980, p. 205, fn. 7) of the educative power of political debate, but it would be implausible to suppose it had no such value. By contrast with citizens of a democracy, those living in a closed society may even be denied the knowledge that alternative policies are conceivable or seriously to be entertained.

What applies in the case of parliamentary democracy applies with even greater force when democracy is of a more directly participatory kind. Here, ordinary citizens are not merely required to consider arguments put forward by potential candidates for office. They actually have to take responsibility for the management of affairs that directly concern them. They are therefore motivated both to inform themselves about the matter in hand and to decide prudently. In participatory democracy citizens are in the position of having to commit themselves publicly both to certain values and to certain assumptions as to how the policies they advocate will work out. However hypocritical or evasive they may be about their reasons for supporting the policies they do, the policies they actually decide upon will be put into practice and will stand or fall on their merits.

A third possible link between education and democracy is contained in the proposition that education is itself an essentially democratic activity. Such a claim would doubtless be dismissed with scorn by some educational philosophers (see Wilson and Cowell, 1983, for example). It may also seem surprising after what has been written about the necessary place of authority in education (Pring, 1975) and the 'asymmetric' nature of the teacher–pupil relationship.

Nevertheless, education is democratic to the extent that both teachers and pupils are subject to the canons of whatever discipline is being explored. A good argument or a relevant piece of evidence is still as good or relevant when brought forward by a mediocre student as when the same argument or evidence is produced by an outstandingly well qualified teacher. Socrates might have argued with a slave about geometry even though he would no doubt have expected unquestioning obedience in the matter of some household chore. Ultimately the aim of the teacher, in so far as he is an educator and not an indoctrinator, ought to be to free his pupils from dependence on his authority, and enable them to become his equals.

This does not, of course, mean that no successfully educated person ever believes anything he is told unless he finds it out for himself. It simply means that he retains the awareness that supposedly true statements are susceptible to independent checking – in principle by anyone. With the possible exception of such special cases as the members of some religions, no one is obliged to believe anything simply on the authority of others.

Other connections between education and democracy have been suggested by Dewey (1916, pp. 81–99) who holds that an activity is both educational and democratic if (i) it concerns the common interest and (ii) it involves many contacts with a wide variety of individuals. It is also inherent in Dewey's views of both education and democracy that these essentially involve a pragmatic problem-solving approach to life, rather than relying on authority or tradition.

It is not clear, however, whether Dewey is pointing to connections between the actual concepts of education and democracy or whether he is advocating a particular kind of education in view of the condition and requirements of American democracy as he saw it at a particular time. It is not obvious that all educational achievements are directly related to the common good or are best acquired through diverse and frequent contact with others. Skilled performance in music, for example, may serve as public entertainment but this is a by-product rather than the point of musical education. Such skill would seem more likely to be acquired under the close tutelage of one or two dedicated teachers than through a variety of more ephemeral contacts. Though it is hoped that the pupil will eventually internalise his own musical standards and thus become free of his teacher's guidance, it is not clear that this is properly conceived as 'problem-solving' in the way that a joiner in a non-traditional society independently finds out for himself how best to put together a serviceable stool.

## Democracy and Liberal Education

It is sometimes suggested (O'Hear, 1981, pp. 15–28) that liberal education is undemocratic because of the stress it places on excellence which, so the argument goes, can by definition only be achieved by the few. This view seems to arise from a number of misconceptions. First, let us deal with the purely logical point that excellence can only be achieved by the few because of the very meaning of the word. This seems to be a case of confusing meaning with etymology. 'Excellent' is a word of high praise, but it does not seem to me that in ordinary and perfectly proper usage it retains its connection in meaning with the verb 'to excel'. Two people may make an excellent job of painting a door or playing a flute solo, without either excelling the other. Indeed, there is no contradiction in saying that on a particular occasion all the instrumentalists in an orchestra performed excellently, even though the orchestra was very large.

It is true that we should not describe some performances as excellent if there had not at some time been other performances that were not excellent. But this is a feature of all adjectives. We should not describe a performance as middling if there were no performances that were not middling, or a door as red if there were no doors that were not red. There are, of course, adjectives that can logically only be ascribed to a small number of individuals. These include such adjectives as 'exceptional', 'unusual', 'extraordinary' and 'unique'. However, I do not think it can be said that liberal education is essentially concerned with pursuing the unique, the extraordinary, or even the exceptional. On the contrary, schools that pride themselves on the high quality of the education they provide characteristically speak of the high *standards* of excellence they set and achieve. This would seem to imply not only that substantial numbers of their pupils do excellent work but that, indeed, all are really expected to do so.

It is nevertheless the case that the worthwhile activities and modes of inquiry that go to make up a liberal education are things that can be done well or badly. It also seems to be a matter of empirical fact (though not of logic) that given any such kind of activity, some will perform better or worse than others, while the great majority will turn in something ranging from passable to very satisfactory. But to see the purpose of choosing educational activities involving standards and gradations of performance as being to distinguish talented from less talented individuals is to miss the point – as well as devaluing the worthy achievements of those whose learning, without being outstanding, is perfectly sound. The point of standards in a liberal education is rather that, once having got someone engaged in an activity which admits of gradations in the quality of performance, one may then hold up the standards inherent in the activity as a guide and model for his own greater efforts and improvement and eventually perhaps as a ground for his justified satisfaction. Beating one's rivals may be a useful source of extrinsic motivation and even personal pleasure but it is neither the point nor the definition of excellence in any academic or cultured pursuit.

That excellence is not of itself inimical to democracy is suggested by the fact that democrats do not seem unduly worried by athletic and other sports in which some are bound to be winners and others losers. Nor does democracy seem threatened by the recognition of really outstanding achievements by Nobel prizewinners and the like. We may all take a disinterested pride in the academic and cultural achievements of other human beings, whether or not these are of benefit to us personally.

What is objectionable to the democrat is not the pursuit of excellence at all but the use of gradations in performance all the way down the line to legitimate a distribution of this world's goods which is widely recognised as unjust. It is certainly not *excellence* in history, mathematics, or English that licenses us to label one child as a future labourer and another as a future white-collar worker or middle manager.

## Democracy and Teaching Styles

There is little that is new to be said under this heading. Educationists have always been critical of harsh or authoritarian teaching styles, on grounds of both humanity and efficiency. Subjection to authoritarian teaching styles seems a singularly inappropriate preparation for life in a democracy. This is not merely an unsubstantiated empirical claim as Wilson and Cowell imply (1983, p. 112). It is first and foremost a value judgement – which if it may be challenged, may also be defended –

about how future democrats and equals ought to be treated. In the absence of evidence to the contrary, however, it also seems likely that citizens capable, individually and collectively, of taking charge of their own lives will be produced by styles emphasising self-directed activity and co-operation rather than by those in which the teacher, clothed in the manner and mantle of authority, harangues the silent and resentful multitude.

## Democracy and the Content of Education

Does commitment to democracy imply a preference for any particular educational content? Are there things which everyone in a democracy needs to learn? Doubtless one obvious candidate for compulsory inclusion is some form of specifically political education. But this topic requires a separate chapter of its own. For the moment I propose to consider only those parts of the curriculum which are normally regarded as not being specifically political.

A particular feature of political decisions as opposed to various kinds of technical decision is that there is no limit to the kind of consideration that may be relevant. The ways in which considerations drawn from many disciplines may be relevant to discussion of the building and routing of a motorway or the privatisation of an industrial concern are too obvious to need spelling out. From this would seem to follow the now orthodox view that all future citizens of a democracy ought to receive some introduction to the various modes of understanding and evaluation at our disposal (P. White, 1971, pp. 23–4).

We saw in Chapter 5 that the content of the curriculum followed by different pupils should not be such as to favour undemocratic tendencies in our society by producing distinct and separate groups of adults with little in common as regards experience and understanding of the world, and predestining some to high- and some to low-status social positions. It was argued in that chapter that there should be a sufficient number of things known and valued by all members of society for the notion of a common interest to be possible.

The content of education in a democracy must, however, also be of relevance to the lives and experience of all children. It is sometimes said – no doubt with justice – that in the past the mass of children were given a watered-down version of the academic curriculum suitable for a cultured and leisured social elite. Bantock's suggestion (1968, pp. 1–43) that certain kinds of knowledge were unsuitable for some children and should not be made available to them is scarcely acceptable in a democracy.

No doubt the way some academic and literary subjects were taught in the past, and still are in some places, was such as to render them meaningless to most pupils. At best they can have been seen by conscientious children as things one ought to learn because they are known by educated people. To such children the possession of certain kinds of knowledge – the grammar of a foreign language, history, the rudiments of how to play a musical instrument – can often have been little more than the badge of a certain social status, rather than something which illuminated the child's experience or increased the range of his activities.

The mastery of such subjects may be the way some working-class children opt for and achieve a measure of social mobility. Under such circumstances schooling must be an irrelevance to the remainder. It is difficult to see how a democrat can accept either the principle of such a filtering process or the idea that the majority of children are to sit through some eleven years of schooling which are not geared to their aims and purposes, but to the maintenance of a system of social stratification which works to their disadvantage.

The criticism may be made that little is being said that would provide any specific material for someone engaged in designing a curriculum. To some extent this will be remedied in Chapter 8 when detailed proposals regarding political education are considered. It should not be too surprising, however, if outside this area, commitment to democracy has little in the way of positive implications for the content of the curriculum. To be committed to democracy is not to be committed to holding that particular policies or even a particular conception of the good should be pursued in the state as a whole. Rather it lays down, in a general way, limits to which the manner in which things are decided must conform.

In much the same way, democracy makes few specific demands regarding the content of education, other than those of a general and procedural kind, such as that knowledge should be presented as something relevant to us all, and as something which, in principle, all can check and generate for themselves. It has been argued (Peters, 1979) that democracy which is the mutual accommodation of equals must depend heavily on discussion. This in turn suggests that in a democracy educators should emphasise the values essential to discussion such as impartiality, respect for others, concern for truth, relevance, evidence, and the like.

Peters suggests that these are 'basic values distinctive to the type of democratic society in which we live' (1979, p. 468), as if in other types of society other educational aims and emphases might be appropriate. This seems a dangerous line of argument, for it appears to suggest that though truth and so on matter in Britain or France they are not quite so important in the education of young people in South Africa or Chile.

Argument about definitions may be sterile and we ought no doubt to beware of smuggling value judgements into stipulative definitions of education. Yet it is far from clear that the teaching of a system of beliefs without emphasising the importance of truth, evidence and criticism can be described as education except in a rather extended sense.

There is a final and not entirely unrelated consideration. If there are special reasons why both truth and the means of distinguishing truth from falsehood matter in the education of future citizens of a democracy, then the distinction between education and indoctrination (see J. White, 1970; also Degenhardt, 1976) becomes particularly crucial. Nothing need be said of the incompatibility between democracy and the deliberate indoctrination of future citizens. Someone committed to democracy, however, might be particularly sensitive to the possibilities of unintentional indoctrination through the content of the curriculum, especially in a society which is as yet far from democratic.

To mention some often-quoted examples, it is just possible that in the past history syllabuses have been excessively ethnocentric or have concentrated unduly on male line genealogies of royal and noble families. Possibly teaching the Tudors and Stuarts and giving only passing mention to the Russian Revolution or the appalling social conditions under early capitalism have been favourable to the status quo. Certain kinds of social education may also be thought to present our existing arrangements as a kind of ultimate reality rather than as a matter of human contrivance subject to criticism and change. Bruner's multi-media MACOS (Man a Course of Study) which continues to be used in some schools in Britain may indirectly teach such values as toughness and survival in a difficult environment as if they were as basic to human as to animal societies.

Once again, however, it is a matter of fine and, some would hold, sterile distinction as to whether the avoidance of such misleading impressions is definitive of history, social studies, or whatever, properly taught, or whether it is simply something favourable to democracy which democrats are keen to smuggle into their definition of educational activities.

# 8

# *Political Education in a Democracy*

Many readers will know that there is no established tradition of specifically political education in British schools. It is true that in the 1930s when, as now, the idea of democracy was thought to be to some extent under threat, there were those who favoured some kind of 'education for citizenship'. But apart from that, the idea received little support until the late 1960s (Heater, 1977a, pp. 27–9). There appear to have been two reasons for this neglect.

First, the notion of political education was often associated with the political indoctrination of totalitarian regimes. Those favouring political education are still often accused of favouring left-wing indoctrination. Secondly, it may with some reason have been thought that with the voting age at 21 and the school-leaving age at 14 or 15 politics had little to do with the condition of childhood and was just not a suitable school subject. Where such subjects as civics or British constitution were taught, this was usually in a very descriptive way, concentrating for the most part on institutions and procedures, rather than on political ideas or controversial issues.

Things changed rather dramatically during the late 1960s and early 1970s. With the school-leaving age now at 16 and the voting age at 18, the prospect of exercising the vote was no longer so distant. It was also felt important at that time to provide a curriculum clearly oriented towards adult life for those who would be staying on into the fifth year for the first time. At this period, too, pupils were beginning to show that they regarded political affairs as anything but irrelevant to them. Studies of political socialisation (Greenstein, 1965; Jaros, 1973) also suggested that this process began fairly early and that political orientations, once taken on, tended to be fairly stable.

The Politics Association, a professional association of teachers of politics in schools and colleges, was founded in 1969 and its journal *Teaching Politics* is now well established. In 1974 the association, jointly with the Hansard Society for Parliamentary Government, received a grant from the Nuffield Foundation to launch a Programme for Political Education. The Hansard Society was also awarded a grant from the Leverhulme Trust to make and publish a survey of levels of political knowledge and ignorance among school-leavers, and a Political Education Research Unit was set up at the University of York. In 1977 Her Majesty's Inspectors of Schools published a discussion paper entitled 'Political Competence' as part of the document *Curriculum 11–16* (DES/HMI, 1977).

More recent official publications have given the subject less prominence (Crick and Porter, 1981) but continue, if with some reluctance, to acknowledge the necessity of work in this area as part of the curriculum of schools and colleges of further education.

The survey of levels of political knowledge and political ignorance and the work of the Programme for Political Education are adequately and accessibly described elsewhere (Stradling, 1977; Crick and Heater, 1977; Crick and Porter, 1978; Brennan, 1981). Frequent reference will necessarily be made to these works in the pages that follow. My main purpose, however, will be to consider certain philosophical questions relating to political education, particularly in the light of the discussion of democracy in Chapters 1–3.

## Is There a Case for Political Education?

The suggestion in Chapter 7 that all or any categories of knowledge may have a part to play in the consideration of a political issue may tempt one to believe that no specifically political education is necessary even in a democracy. It might perhaps be thought that what is required is a good general education coupled with sound common sense and a degree of fair-mindedness.

In small, relatively homogeneous independent communities this might well be true. The affairs of such communities would be likely to be simple and the effects of decisions taken on the interests of individuals would be relatively obvious. Any necessary political skills and the knowledge required to exercise them could no doubt be picked up informally. The view that a specifically political education is unnecessary may fairly readily be reconciled with the classical theory of democracy as it prevailed up to the end of the nineteenth century.

Issues which in any way concerned the elector may have seemed relatively simple and straightforward whether or not they were so in fact. The suffrage was then more or less limited to people whose background and way of life provided a degree of political knowledge and experience.

If political education is conceived of as coming to understand political issues and learning to take part in political activities, then holders of the alternative or elitist theory of democracy would be bound to regard it as unnecessary, not to say positively undesirable for the mass of the population. If the electorate is simply to choose between different groups of leaders and entrust the business of government to them, too much knowledge of political issues and too much understanding of the political process might give its members ideas above their station. As will be seen, however, there may be versions of political education that alternative theorists would find less objectionable.

It might also be thought that proponents of participatory democracy who stressed the importance of citizen participation at local and community level would not be too concerned with political education which related to central government and higher levels of the state bureaucracy. This, however, would be a mistake, for the satisfactory outcome of even local controversies may often depend on national policies, or the ability to bring influence to bear at many political and administrative levels.

In this chapter it will be argued that in any democracy justified in terms of the right of individuals to equal influence in public affairs there is, given the complexities of modern issues and the remoteness of modern democratic government, a very strong case for a specifically political component in the education of the young. Such a component, it will be argued, is justified on both educational and political grounds.

## Educational Grounds

If a future citizen were destined to play no active part in the political world, even to the extent of apathetically casting his quinquennial vote, there would still be a strong educational case for providing him with a measure of political education in the sense of a knowledge and understanding of the political process, and some of the issues with which it deals.

The political world is a very important part of the environment in which the individual lives. Many of the things he undertakes and more especially many of the things that befall him will only be fully comprehensible in political terms. The acts of joining Her Majesty's Forces, dedicating oneself to public service, or even things like taking part or not taking part in a strike are all understood more fully when seen in their political perspective. If the pupil is later unemployed, sent to fight in distant parts of the world, or arrested, these events may be susceptible of political explanation, as may the very nature of the school in which he now finds himself.

The media too provide an important part of the individual's experience, and are much concerned with political figures and political activity. Yet the presentation of these may not be such that young people are able to derive much knowledge and understanding from them without possessing some basic conceptual framework and previous knowledge relating to political matters. This is borne out by Stradling's findings (1977, pp. 27–8) that a good number of young people do read newspapers, albeit in the majority of cases the popular press, and also spend time watching television newscasts. Yet the survey also shows that they derive very little political knowledge and understanding from these activities.

Political knowledge and therefore political education call on and therefore contribute to the development of many disciplines. Prominent among these is moral reasoning, for many political judgements are about the ultimate values people hold. Centrally, however, political understanding is part of the understanding of one's own and other minds. Political activity is an important human activity, arguably even an essential human activity without which someone is less than human. It is part of our social understanding, that is, our understanding of society. It clearly has links with economics and, through the statistics which play an important part in modern political discussion, with mathematics.

Besides its traditional links with history, attention has also been drawn to political education's link with English and communications. Many English literary works, both modern ones and the older classics, can only be understood fully if the reader has some understanding of the political implications of their background and content. There is also the point that arguing a case of a broadly political kind with which the pupil feels involved is an exercise frequently used – at least at the level of further education – as a means of extending his skills in oral and written communication.

Given these links with other subjects, it is sometimes suggested, especially by schools and local education authorities (DES/WO, 1979, p. 160), that the requirement that pupils should receive some form of political education is adequately met by its introduction into other timetable subjects. While Stradling (1977, pp. 51–7) recognises that valuable opportunities for the development of political literacy do exist in the teaching of other subjects, he argues that this, in itself, is insufficient. In his view the political education of pupils is more likely to be carried out in accordance with professional standards of objectivity and competence generally if specific timetable provision is made, explicit syllabuses are written and ultimately qualified teachers of politics are appointed. Stradling's survey may be taken to show fairly convincingly that the indirect approach to the imparting of political understanding, at least as far as current issues are concerned, has not proved very effective to date.

## Political Grounds

From earlier chapters it will be clear that the democrat is committed not only to a wider diffusion of political knowledge and understanding but, as far as is practicable, to an equalisation of influence on collective policies. Some people in our society, whether through family background or formal education, do have very considerable knowledge of how power is exercised in our society and how to accede to positions in which they themselves may come to exercise power and influence. For the democrat as defined in Chapter 4, there would seem to be strong arguments for spreading this knowledge as widely as possible, for the voter who does not know what politics is about or what the policies of various parties are and what these policies entail cannot exercise his minimum right of voting at elections to advantage.

## Political Education and Indoctrination

Before leaving the question of the desirability of specific timetable provision for political education, something needs to be said about the widespread anxiety felt by teachers and education authorities that political education may be, or may be mistaken for, indoctrination. The term political education and its equivalents certainly have a bad reputation as a result of their use under totalitarian regimes, not to mention efforts in the United States to instil patriotism and commitment to the American way of life into American citizens of diverse cultural origins.

In so far as objections to political education merit discussion and are not simply expressions of administrators' and politicians' desires not to rock the boat, they are of three kinds:

(1)   Political education, unless it is purely descriptive of institutions as civics and British constitution were often supposed to be, is a matter not of fact but of value, so that whatever is contained in a political education syllabus will be inherently indoctrinatory. People who take this view may add that political education, like sectarian religion, ought to be undertaken either by the family or by political organisations, and left severely alone by school-teachers.

(2)   The notion of the political is an essentially contested concept.

This means that what is and what is not political is itself a political issue. Consequently there is no possibility of agreement as to what may legitimately be included in a political education syllabus.

(3) Even if the above two objections are somehow met and politics is allowed in schools at all, the temptation for individual teachers to influence their pupils will be very great, and not easy to detect. It is therefore easier by far to issue a blanket prohibition 'No politics!' so that anyone talking about politics at all, however disinterestedly, is automatically out of line. The tendency of prudent heads to think in this way is reinforced by the consideration that even if teachers succeed in presenting political issues in a balanced way, this is no guarantee that the school will not still be accused of bias. In political matters, one man's moderation may be another's extremism.

In reply to these particular anxieties it is appropriate to begin by making the general observation that both teachers and educationists are far less anxious than they used to be about the bogeyman of indoctrination. To begin with, it is no longer widely believed that 'facts' are the only things which it is respectable to pass on to children in an educational context, and open and visible teaching of values is no longer universally regarded as indoctrinatory in itself. Many people now reserve this term for teaching (whether of facts or of values) in such a way that the pupil is not easily able to question what he is taught (see J. White, 1970).

Crick (1977) argues quite convincingly that much teaching about political issues may be thoroughly factual. This includes information about what the currently controversial political issues are, who holds certain views and how people's interests might be affected by their implementation. On his view it is no part of the teacher's job to attempt to influence pupils' substantive political views. Rather, he sees it as part of political education to present contrary views with empathy so that even when they are rejected it remains possible to see how they can plausibly and honourably be held.

Let it be added that even if discussion of political matters is or risks being indoctrinatory, it is no solution simply to avoid such discussion in school altogether. To leave someone in a state of ignorance or error may be every bit as much a biased act as telling him something. This will be particularly obvious if it is thought that, as is often argued, the ignorance or 'false consciousness' of the people is more favourable to some interests than to others.

That 'the political' is an essentially contested concept in the manner indicated is more of a theoretical than a practical problem. There are many issues that are widely agreed to be political in both a broad and a narrow sense. If it is thought by some people to be a matter of controversy how industry should be run or military forces deployed, then these issues ought to be included (rather than excluded) when a course of political education is being planned. To attempt to put one's important interests out of the political firing-line, or to concentrate attack on what the opposition regards as safe positions, are tactics of political debate which future citizens ought to be taught to recognise.

That political education on the timetable may be a temptation to some would-be indoctrinators cannot be denied. If, however, the social, political and economic conditions of the adult world are to be discussed with pupils at all – and it is difficult to argue that they should not be – then this would seem to be an argument for having the subject taught openly and explicitly. In this way, everything is above board. Attainments can perfectly properly be assessed and teaching inspected. Under these circumstances, too, teaching is likely to be carried out by those properly qualified in the subject, who may be expected to have some loyalty to canons of truth and judgement in that area rather than to merely substantive political opinions.

If no explicit or disciplined political education takes place in schools, pupils will certainly continue to acquire political views, but from individuals and organisations that may feel no commitment to the ideals of objectivity, the empathic presentation of alternative views, or a careful, well-substantiated, or even truthful presentation of the facts.

The position of schools that wish to introduce some form of explicitly political education is now rather easier than it was. Politics is now established as a fairly reputable area of study at universities and some other institutions in higher education. The Politics Association and the Programme for Political Education are in good standing, and have shown with some degree of plausibility how the subject can be taught in an intellectually honest form at school and further education levels. Headteachers, furthermore, are no longer held solely responsible for the curriculum of their schools in quite the way they were before the so-called Great Debate of 1976. Her Majesty's Inspectorate and the Department of Education and Science have attempted to give some curricular guidelines and have encouraged local education authorities to do the same. The head who includes political education on his curriculum may at least point to some official encouragement for his policies, however muted and inexplicit this encouragement may be.

## What Kind of Political Education?

It is not here proposed to advocate a particular style of political education. The term has received a number of interpretations and is subject to on-going discussion and controversy in many quarters. It may therefore be helpful to distinguish critically between some of these interpretations.

## Teaching Respect for Democracy

This was the interpretation of the term adopted by many people writing before and shortly after the Second World War. Nazis and communists had 'educated' their young people politically and it was felt that Britain should do the same in order to defend its democratic values and way of life against subversion. This form of political education resembles indoctrination in that it is carried out with the intention that pupils should emerge with certain more or less unshakeable beliefs, values and attitudes. Besides the view that democracy, especially the British parliamentary form of democracy, is the only acceptable form of polity, teaching of this kind may stress such democratic values as respect for 'law and order' and for 'democratically elected authorities'. It will doubtless also emphasise the duties and above all the responsibilities rather than the rights of citizens in a democracy. This concept of political education is the only one countenanced as at all acceptable for the majority of children by the Norwood Committee (Board of Education, 1943, pp. 57–9, quoted in Brennan, 1981, p. 39). It is, of course, also the one most likely to recommend itself to holders of the alternative theory of democracy.

## Civics and British Constitution

A purely descriptive approach to the teaching of politics is criticised by Crick (1969) on both intellectual and pedagogic grounds. Intellectually, talk of institutions, procedures, details of local government powers, the relationship between local and central government, and so on, is misleading if these things are discussed in abstraction from the interests and issues with which they are designed to deal. Inevitably such an approach gives the impression that somewhere there exists, even though not in a written form, something called 'The British Constitution' which ought not to be infringed. Despite efforts to remain in the realm of fact, the impression given is the normative one that to act 'unconstitutionally' is a bad thing.

Pedagogically, Crick claims, such knowledge is inert in the sense that apart from passing an examination there is little the pupil can do with his knowledge. It does not illuminate any aspect of the pupil's life, for this is affected not by institutional rules and procedures but by real politics, the interplay of power and interest. It does not give genuine insight into a mode of human activity, nor does it even provide a valuable academic qualification, for A-level British constitution is not highly esteemed in the universities. Above all, Crick (1969) claims, the subject, at least as taught until recently, is boring. Politics conceived in this way also fails to provide a model for material suitable to pupils over the full range of ability, background and motivation.

### 'Political Literacy'

The term 'political literacy' is used in the papers of the Hansard Society Programme for Political Education, as well as more generally in the writings of Crick, Heater, Porter, Stradling and others associated with the project. This usage has various advantages, some of which are spelled out by Crick and Porter (1978, pp. 30–6). To speak of political literacy avoids much of the odium attaching to the term political education in the past. It expresses the essential modesty of the Hansard Society Working Papers' aim to 'establish the basic requisites and minimum political content for education in secondary schools, colleges of education and non-degree work'. Crick and Porter also claim (p. 31) that the concept of political literacy, which emphasises knowledge, skills and attitudes, is a much broader concept than either 'political competence' or 'political understanding', for it entails possessing not only the 'basic information which is prerequisite to understanding the political dimension of a given context' (p. 39) but also the skills required to influence group decisions and the proclivity to do so in an appropriate way. With literacy proper the term shares the advantage of being a state which may be reached in a number of ways and may in principle be set out in objectives of varying levels and subsequently assessed.

Though stressing that they are not concerned to produce anything resembling a definitive syllabus leading to political literacy, Crick and Porter specify their aims and approach in some detail. Thus, for example, it is specified that a politically literate person will know 'what the main political disputes are about; what beliefs the main contestants have of them and how they are likely to affect him' (p. 33).

Besides a proclivity to try to influence group decisions in ways suggested by his own preferences and principles, it is argued that the politically literate person's attitudes will be governed by certain procedural principles. These are the principles of freedom, fairness, respect for truth, respect for reasoning and toleration which are essential to any attempt to reconcile disputes and conflicts of interest in ways that are equitable and respectful of the sincerity of others. The authors are less specific about the particular skills a politically literate person would have, though it is said that he would be capable of active participation in a democracy and able to devise strategies for influencing and achieving change.

The best approach to the development of political literacy, it is suggested, would be to start from political issues and certainly not from institutions and procedures. Though starting from issues, whether at national or international levels or at the level of the 'politics of everyday life', it is suggested that schools and colleges should aim to establish some form of conceptual and analytical framework which will enable pupils to understand the political world about them. This includes both that part of the everyday world with which they come directly into contact, and that which comes to them though the media. One of the authors suggests (p. 51) some twelve criteria that he regards as basic to our understanding of government, individuals and the relationship between them. He does not, however, regard such a list as necessarily definitive, and other writers associated with the project suggest alternatives (pp. 90–9).

The programme is held to incorporate conservative, liberal and radical elements. It entails knowing and appreciating the value of the present system, the participatory attitudes and skills essential for active citizenship, and consideration of possible changes of direction in government or alternative government systems.

In attempting to assess the political literacy approach to political education, it is clear that the significance of this development cannot be denied. Besides representing a clearly articulated theory of politics and pedagogic rationale, the findings of the working party have been backed up and disseminated by means of a considerable volume of publications. These are not only of a general theoretical kind. There also exists illustrative material in the form of sample syllabuses and teaching units intended for specific levels.

Tribute has been paid to the skill of the proponents of the approach in gaining recognition and acceptance for it (Tapper and Salter, 1978, pp. 68–9). One of its major assets has been its relatively eclectic base. While stressing the conceptual, procedural, issue-centred approach which is the essence of political literacy as conceived of by Crick and his associates, these writers have profited from existing dissatisfaction with the inert knowledge of traditional civics and British constitution. Though stressing that in their view political literacy objectives are most likely to be achieved by means of specific timetable provision, they do not rule out their achievement via the medium of more traditional subjects. They also make a conciliatory gesture in the direction of another tradition in political education (which will be considered below) when it is suggested (Stradling and Porter, 1978, p. 79) that some political skills may best be learned by involvement in school decision-making.

Indeed, the conclusion must be that the political literacy approach embodies the most practical and generally acceptable approach to political education currently available. It is proof against many standard conservative objections for it can no longer be said that politics are not of interest to or in any way the business of pupils in the later years of the secondary school. The large element of factual content, the assertion that it is not the job of teachers to attempt to influence pupils in their substantive beliefs and above all the unimpeachable procedural values the project advocates should recommend the scheme to all but extreme reactionaries who object to the dissemination of any political understanding and know-how at all among the populace.

There do, however, appear to be two lines of criticism which must be taken account of. The first of these is raised by Stradling (1977, p. 48) who is generally favourable to the political literacy approach, and is a contributor to Crick and Porter (1968). Stradling points out that the politically literate person described by Crick and others would, for example, 'understand and use those political concepts minimally necessary to construct simple conceptual and analytic frameworks' and that such an achievement 'presupposes to some extent the use of an elaborated code by the student'. On the basis of his empirical researches Stradling suggests the possibility that 'teachers in attempting to develop political literacy in the classroom may be using an elaborated code of language for which many of their pupils have no equivalent response' (p. 45).

It would, of course, be an obvious defect in any educational programme if it were intellectually inaccessible to large numbers of those for whom it was intended. It would be a particularly grave defect in a programme of political education in a democracy whose proponents were committed to the view that one should aim to enable all to acquire political skills and understandings in order that all might exert their due portion of influence in political matters. By implication, the effect of such a programme could only be to convince many pupils, especially those from certain social strata, that such things were 'too difficult' or not for them and were best left to those more able to grasp them.

This depressing conclusion is not inevitable, however. It is certainly not the contention of Bernstein, the originator of the terms 'restricted' and 'elaborated codes', that working-class children are congenitally or permanently incapable of acquiring either the capacity to use elaborated codes of language or a capacity for abstract thought. What Bernstein does argue is that to an observably significant degree middle-class children do happen to use what he calls an elaborated code more frequently than working-class children. This is presumably because they have had greater opportunities for acquiring such a mode of expression in the course of their previous experience.

Now if the ability to handle this style of expression and the mode of thought which Stradling assumes to go with it is acquired by use, this is not an argument for continuing to deprive working-class pupils of contact with activities in which elaborated codes find their natural home. Indeed, quite the contrary policy would seem to follow, though familiarity with Bernstein's work would help to sensitise the teacher to the difficulties some of his pupils would experience.

The second objection to the Hansard Society's Programme of Political Education is of a more radical kind. It is true that the programme is not obviously biased in favour of conservatism or elitist conceptions of democracy in the way that 'education for citizenship' is often held to be. Nevertheless, its conception of politics as the 'process through which conflicts of interests and values within a group are *conciliated*' (my emphasis) makes it naturally suspect to the radical, as does the importance it attaches to individuality and rights and the procedural values of freedom, truth, reason, and above all, toleration. These procedures, Tapper and Salter argue, 'bias the political process in favour of certain groups' (1978, p. 74) and to insist upon such procedures as if they were ultimate values 'cannot but help to place societies like our own in a comparatively favourable light'. The Programme for Political Education, Tapper and Salter claim, is at best reformist rather than radical. They also imply that the 'true intentions' of Crick and his associates are 'cementing the established order' and 'the shoring up of the present society' (ibid., p. 73).

Leaving aside the 'true intentions' of all concerned, I propose to consider only the claim that the Programme for Political Education is reformist and that it serves to cement the established order. As regards 'reformism', it must be noted that in the radical vocabulary this denotes not the gradual improvement of society, but merely the pretence of gradual improvement while leaving major inequalities unaffected. It is an item of faith among some radicals that such inequalities cannot be removed in a piecemeal fashion, but only by revolution.

What does seem possible is that a programme of political education of the kind here under consideration would, if effective, delay or even prevent violent confrontation between government and a disaffected populace. It might do this by fostering the belief that there are ways other than by violent confrontation of changing the way the world is and improving one's lot. Many people outside the radical tradition mentioned above are probably in some uncertainty as to whether this belief is true or false. Of course, no one but a blind fool would think that the world as it is is perfectly just and ought not to be changed. But even if it is less than perfect, the question is still to be asked whether revolution is a good way of improving it, or the course of action most in the interests of most people. If, in the end, gradual reform, of which the political education of the younger generation may be seen as an aspect, turns out to be futile, then obviously we shall be faced with a straight

100

choice between revolution (and therefore educational procedures likely to bring it about) and grinning and bearing the situation as it is. But it is far from clear that the possibility of alternative means to the desired end is as yet fully exhausted and, along with other measures, political education of a non-revolutionary kind would at least seem to merit a try.

## School Democracy as a Means of Political Education

School democracy as a morally and politically appropriate mode of school organisation was considered in an earlier chapter. At that point it was argued that though some functions of school management ought to undergo a degree of democratisation, the extent to which this would be appropriate was limited by the purposes for which schools exist, the nature of the pedagogic relationship between teachers and pupils, and the relative immaturity and dependence of the latter. At that point one particular line of argument in favour of pupil power was deliberately left unexamined. This was the argument that such an arrangement would prove a valuable means of political education.

In the late 1960s and early 1970s this argument in favour of school democracy was not infrequently put forward alongside more strident and contentious (though not necessarily invalid) arguments based on the supposed rights of children. There exist two relatively substantial and careful works (Entwistle, 1971, and Ungoed-Thomas, 1972) urging the use of democratic activity among pupils as a means of political education.

Ungoed-Thomas's book *Our School* is subtitled *A Handbook on the Practice of Democracy by Secondary School Pupils* and indicates many practical ways in which democratic activity may be encouraged at school level. Entwistle stresses the importance of associational democracy in voluntary organisations in the everyday life of citizens, and argues that this rather than the macro-level parliamentary democracy should provide the model for pupil participation in the management of schools.

In seeing the actual participation of pupils in the running of some of their own affairs as necessary to political education, Ungoed-Thomas, Entwistle and other writers adopting their point of view can point to distinguished philosophical antecedents. Mill (1861, p. 223) regarded self-government in voluntary organisations and local government as the means by which a people might gain the experience necessary for self-government nationally. Oakeshott (1962, pp. 111–36) may also be cited in support of the claim that political understanding is not to be gained in the classroom or lecture-room alone but requires the practice of actual political activity as well.

Nevertheless, a number of caveats are to be entered regarding this mode of political education, particularly if it is thought that the whole task is to be achieved by pupil participation alone, whether in the actual task of running school affairs or through participation in mock activities such as mock elections, mock trials, mock public meetings, and so on.

The most obvious and cogent reservation to be made is that pupils are only 'playing at politics' and are not engaged in real politics at all, for real politics is about power upon which real and important differences of outcome may depend. This is most apparent in the case of such activities as mock elections, and so on. Though these may be taken quite seriously by the pupils themselves they have the effect of concentrating attention upon the procedures of voting, listening to and possibly making political speeches.

Though these activities are an important element in the working of Western democracies, undue emphasis on them may distract attention from something more fundamental, namely, the central role of discussion aimed at conciliation and the need of individuals in a democracy to make responsible decisions which they themselves may have to play some part in carrying out, or by which they themselves may be affected.

The possibility of setting up school councils is discussed by both Entwistle and, especially, Ungoed-Thomas. Such councils already exist in many schools and vary in their composition. Some may have a majority of pupil representatives, others may have equal numbers of pupils and staff. Some may include representatives of auxiliary employees, others not. Often genuine attempts are made to provide these bodies with real responsibilities about which to decide. This, however, is not easy since, as we saw in Chapter 6, headteachers and staff cannot actually divest themselves of responsibility in matters of any importance.

School councils often fall into disuse through lack of business. They may also engender cynicism when sophisticated and critical pupils point to the relative triviality of the business placed before them and the limits placed on their powers by the fact that real responsibility, and therefore real power, lies with adults. This criticism should, however, be treated with some caution. The objection that school councils have 'no real power' because they cannot change the school syllabus or sack the headteacher is not valid, for as we saw earlier all democratic bodies are limited by their terms of reference. There is nevertheless a practical problem of keeping the council supplied with appropriate business once the original enthusiasm of head, staff and pupils has waned. School authorities might, however, make greater efforts in this direction if the council's activities and other aspects of school democracy were seen as part of the educational process, rather than as a reluctant concession to pupil agitation.

A more radical objection to school councils is that they do not provide education in participant democracy at all, but education in leadership for the few and political quietism for the many, that is, it is the wrong sort of political education. Force is given to this objection by the fact that, unlike parliamentary and local government elections, it is rarely the case that candidates for school office are able to present alternative policies between which their electorate may choose. Voters therefore simply have to choose the 'best person' to represent them in the best traditions of democracy in its elitist form.

If the school council is to be of any use for the purposes of political education it must at very least be backed up by other, lower-level democratic arrangements in other parts of the school's life. Steps also need to be taken to make known the work and decisions of the council and actively canvass opinion on some issues before it. The school council would be no more than an ornament if the general atmosphere of the school were authoritarian and pupils were expected to take no active part in the discussion of how things were to be arranged either in the classroom or in the running of out-of-school activities.

However democratically a school is run, it is impossible to suppose that this in itself would meet the needs of its pupils' political education. It is not obvious that the knowledge and skills needed if citizens are to play their democratic part in running the affairs of a modern industrial state are the same as those that can be acquired by participating in the management of limited aspects of a school's life. The differences between the two may be thought to be ones not of scale but of kind.

The citizen is relatively unlikely to meet his MP far less a member of his government, except perhaps briefly at election time on his doorstep. He may feel he knows his MP through seeing and hearing him on television, but increasingly the public image of politicians projected by the media is carefully managed. Even in a large school, by contrast, pupils have some feeling of belonging to the same face-to-face community. Also, the effect of decisions by the school council or other responsible group of pupils on the life of an individual may be relatively small. The adult school hierarchy, his parents and other out-of-school contacts may loom far larger in his consciousness, whereas the citizen's existence is wholly within the ambit of the state. The state has powers of coercion and ultimately the power of life and death over citizens. Political decisions may have very great importance for the lives, happiness and prosperity of individual members of the state.

For these reasons we may be in some doubt as to how far political experience at the micro level of the school is a satisfactory preparation for activity at the much more complex and daunting level of the state. Certainly some activity extending pupils' knowledge and providing information about actual current issues in the adult world would seem a necessary supplement.

## Community Action – Unmasking the True Nature of the Power Structure

Some radical writers claim that political education in the classroom and 'playing at democracy' in the school are not only ineffectual modes of political education; they are, it is claimed, actually worse than useless in that they shore up the existing situation by disguising the true extent of the individual's powerlessness. Such writers may claim that political education is only likely to take place when pupils attempt to undertake something within the community and are confronted by the resistance of those who hold power, either in the community or nationally. People are then forced to recognise the sham nature of gradualist institutions, which are blocked as soon as they attempt to bring about real changes in the community's distribution of power and wealth. And it is at that point that a revolutionary state of mind may be engendered.

For example, a school community service unit may begin by helping old age pensioners to tidy up their gardens or decorate their houses. Its efforts will no doubt be praised on speech day and similar occasions. But if pupils, egged on by their teachers, decide to 'help the elderly' by publicising the squalid conditions in which they live, or the failure of the council or private landlords to carry out repairs to which the old people are legally entitled, the response may be different. It is at this point, according to the mythology, that phones begin to ring, the teacher in charge of the unit is called to the headteacher's study and the unit is either disbanded or has its efforts directed elsewhere.

No doubt involvement in such an experience would prove an invaluable piece of political education for the pupils involved if they became aware of just what had gone on behind the scenes and why, and if they were fully cognisant of the motives of the teacher by whom the incident had been orchestrated. But at best this must be an essentially one-off experience. Such events depend on a happy coincidence of circumstances and staff commitment. They cannot be relied on to provide the staple introduction to the understanding of our society which is needed by all pupils if they are to comprehend fully the course of their own lives and the events that befall them.

Setting aside the question of social action as a practicable teaching method, however, ought not the aim of political education to be the 'unmasking' of social inequalities and the encouragement of political activism? Should not inequalities of income, class-differentiated access to educational opportunity, sexual and social discrimination, poverty, and so on, all figure largely in any programme of political education? Of course, some aspects of our society may be a cause for satisfaction rather than the reverse. There can be no question of indoctrinating our pupils. Respect for their autonomy does not allow us to present biased information or use emotional language in an attempt to hasten the more or less dramatic social change which *we* know to be desirable. But in so far as the inequalities and injustices referred to above are indeed important features of the society in which our pupils will grow up, it is difficult to argue that teachers should disguise the fact.

Such is the idealism of youth that some of our pupils will be indignant, and determine that the present state of things is not worthy of them or their generation.

Can it be the teacher's duty to persuade them otherwise?

# Suggestions for Further Reading

Full details of all works referred to in this and earlier parts of the book are given in the Bibliography.

## Democracy (Chapters 1–3)

The major classical works of Hobbes, Locke, Rousseau, Burke, Paine and Mill are all widely available in modern editions, some of which are indicated in the Bibliography. Readers will probably find Locke (1690) and Mill (1861, chs 1–9) particularly illuminating as the theoretical bases of Western liberal democratic theory, though the main works of all the writers mentioned remain remarkably accessible and pertinent to contemporary questions.

Lindsay's short work (1929) provides a good introduction to the classical theory of democracy. Short overview accounts of democratic theory are contained in Macpherson (1966), Margolis (1979) and Lively (1975). Of the three, Lively is the most demanding. Macpherson, though less recent, deals particularly well with non-liberal democracy in communist and Third World countries. Singer (1973) and Lucas (1976) also provide acceptable background reading on some of the central problems of democracy. Pateman (1970) discusses classical and alternative theories clearly and critically before moving on to the concept of participatory democracy, which is his main concern. Megill (1970) treats participatory democracy in a stimulating manner. Schumpeter (1954, see esp. chs 20–23) is a major theoretical exponent of the alternative theory, while Almond and Verba (1965) are widely quoted as providing empirical support for that theory.

## Education as Legitimation (Chapter 4)

Basic texts for the view that education is primarily an instrument of oppression are Althusser (1971), Bourdieu and Passeron (1970) and Bowles and Gintis (1976). Davies (1976) provides a useful overview and many references. The doctrine that education serves to legitimate inequality also underlies the writings of the de-schoolers; see Illich (1971), Lister (n.d.), Reimer (1971), Goodman (1971) and Postman and Weingartner (1971). The view that knowledge is socially determined and therefore to a degree arbitrary is well represented by articles in Young (1971); also by Berger and Luckman (1967).

## Selection and Private Education (Chapter 5)

The partisan works produced in the comprehensive debate – Rubinstein and Stoneman (1970), Benn and Simon (1972) and Cox and Dyson (1971) – are all now somewhat *passé*. Cooper (1980), though not an easy work to read, is a stimulating and valuable critique of the easy progressivism of the 1970s. Cohen (1981) is also intellectually demanding and provides a closely argued defence of private education on ethical grounds. Friedman (1962, ch. 5) and West (1970) set out the historical and economic arguments for vouchers and an expansion of private education.

## The Democratic Government of Education (Chapter 6)

Pamphlets from the National Union of Teachers and Rank and File are useful statements of these two bodies' views at the height of the debate on this topic and are available in many education libraries. Arguments for the involvement of parents, teachers and in some cases pupils in the government of schools are set out in the Taylor Report (DES/WO, 1977). Bridges and Scrimshaw (1975) and Sockett (1980) both contain short readable articles relating to the government of schools and teacher accountability. Watts (1977, ch. 15) discusses the question from a headteacher's point of view. Wringe (1981, chs 1, 14, 17) describes the course of the children's rights controversy between 1968 and 1973 and discusses pupils' rights of participation. Articles by Berg, Neill and Duane in Adams *et al.* (1971) provide a useful background to the question of pupil self-government as, of course, does Neill (1962).

## Democracy and Education (Chapter 7)

References to Mill's views on the relationship between democracy and education are to be found in several of his works (notably 1859, 1861 and 1867). Garforth (1971) is a useful collection of Mill's educational writings containing, among other things, the text of Mill's Inaugural Address at the University of St Andrews in 1867. Two other books by Garforth (1979 and 1980) are systematic studies of aspects of Mill's educational thought. A good indication of Dewey's views on this question is to be found in his *Democracy and Education* (1916, esp. ch. 7). Peters's (1966, pp. 291–320) discussion was for some time regarded as the standard account of the educational implications of democracy. In later studies he establishes the link between education and autonomy (1973) and examines certain educational aims that may be expected to receive particular emphasis in a democracy (1979). Apparent contradictions between education and democracy are discussed by Pring (1975), Scrimshaw (1975) and Olafson (1973).

## Political Education (Chapter 8)

Brennan (1981) is a good readable account of work in this field. The report and papers of the Working Party of the Hansard Society's Programme for

107

Political Education are conveniently brought together in Crick and Porter (1978). Some of the same material is also contained in Heater (1969) and also Crick and Heater (1977). Stradling (1977) gives an account of a survey of the political knowledge of school-leavers in Britain. Criticisms of the Programme for Political Education are to be found in Tapper and Salter (1978, ch. 4) and from a more radical point of view in Whitty (1978). Kingdom (1976) and P. White (1971 and 1979) deal with specifically philosophical aspects of the case for and against political education. P. White (1979) also presents arguments in favour of workplace democracy generally. Entwistle (1971) and Ungoed-Thomas (1972) make the case for a degree of pupil democracy as a means of political education. Entwistle also has useful things to say about associational democracy. Greenstein (1965) and Jaros (1973) are useful introductions to the notion of political socialisation.

# Bibliography

Adams, P., *et al.* (1971), *Children's Rights* (London: Elek).

Aiken, W., and Lafollette, H. (eds) (1980), *Whose Child?* (Totowa, NJ: Littlefield Adams).

Almond, G. A., and Verba, S. (1965), *The Civic Culture* (Boston, Mass.: Little, Brown).

Althusser, L. (1971), 'Ideology and ideological state apparatuses', in Cosin, 1972, pp. 242–80.

Bantock, G. H. (1968), *Culture, Industrialization and Education* (London: Routledge & Kegan Paul).

Bantock, G. H. (1975), 'Equality and education', in B. Wilson, 1975, pp. 110–54.

Benn, C., and Simon, B. (1972), *Half-Way There* (Harmondsworth: Penguin).

Benn, S. I., and Peters, R. S. (1959), *Social Principles and the Democratic State* (London: Allen & Unwin).

Bereiter, C. (1973), *Must We Educate?* (Englewood Cliffs, NJ: Prentice-Hall).

Berelson, B. R., Lazarsfeld, P. F., and McPhee, W. N. (1954), *Voting* (Chicago: University of Chicago Press).

Berg, L. (1971), 'Moving towards self-government', in Adams *et al.*, 1971, pp. 9–50.

Berger, P. L., and Luckman, T. (1967), *The Social Construction of Reality* (Harmondsworth: Penguin).

Bernstein, B. (1961), 'Social class and linguistic development: a theory of social learning', in A. H. Halsey, J. Floud and A. Anderson (eds), *Education, Economy and Society* (New York: The Free Press), pp. 288–314.

Board of Education (1943), *Curriculum and Examinations in Secondary Schools: Report of the Secondary Schools Examination Council under the Chairmanship of Lord Norwood* (London: HMSO).

Bourdieu, P., and Passeron, J.-C. (1970), *La Réproduction*, trans. R. Nice as *Reproduction in Education, Society and Culture* (London and Beverly Hills: Sage, 1977).

Bowles, S., and Gintis, H. (1976), *Schooling in Capitalist America* (London: Routledge & Kegan Paul).

Boyson, R. (1972), *Education: Threatened Standards* (Enfield: Churchill Press).

Brennan, T. (1981), *Political Education and Democracy* (Cambridge: CUP).

Bridges, D., and Scrimshaw, P. (1975), *Values and Authority in Schools* (London: Hodder & Stoughton).

Brown, S. C. (ed.) (1975), *Philosophers Discuss Education* (London: Macmillan).

Burke, E. (1790), *Reflections on the Revolution in France* (Harmondsworth: Penguin, 1968).

Cohen, B. (1981), *Education and the Individual* (London: Allen & Unwin).

Cooper, D. E. (1975), 'Quality and equality in education', in Brown, 1975.

Cooper, D. E. (1980), *Illusions of Equality* (London: Routledge & Kegan Paul).

Cosin, B. R. (ed.) (1972), *Education: Structure and Society* (Harmondsworth: Penguin).

Cox, C. B., and Dyson, A. E. (eds) (1971), *The Black Papers on Education* (London: Davis Poynter).

Crick, B. (1969), 'The introducing of politics', in Heater, 1969, pp. 5–20.

Crick, B. (1977), 'On bias', in Crick and Heater, 1977, pp. 34–50.

Crick, B., and Heater, D. (1977), *Essays on Political Education* (Ringmer: Falmer Press).

Crick, B., and Porter, A. (eds) (1978), *Political Education and Political Literacy* (London: Longman).

Crick, B., and Porter, A. (1981), 'Political education', in J. White *et al.*, 1981, pp. 25–33.

Crosland, C. A. R. (1962), *The Conservative Enemy* (London: Cape).

Dahl, R. (1956), *A Preface to Democratic Theory* (Chicago: University of Chicago Press).

Davies, B. (1976), *Social Control and Education* (London: Methuen).

Degenhardt, M. A. B. (1976), 'Indoctrination', in Lloyd, 1976, pp. 19–25.

DES (Department of Education and Science)/HMI (Her Majesty's Inspectorate) (1977), *Curriculum 11–16* (London: DES).

DES/HMI (1980), *A View of the Curriculum* (London: HMSO).

DES/WO (Welsh Office) (1977), *A New Partnership for our Schools: Report by a Committee of Inquiry appointed by the Secretary of State for Education and Science and the Secretary of State for Wales under the Chairmanship of Mr Tom Taylor, CBE* (London: HMSO).

DES/WO (1979), *Local Authority Arrangements for the School Curriculum: Report of the Circular 14/77 Review* (London: HMSO).

DES/WO (1980), *A Framework for the School Curriculum* (London: DES).

DES/WO (1981), *The School Curriculum* (London: HMSO).

DT (Department of Trade) (1977), *Report of the Committee of Inquiry on Industrial Democracy under the Chairmanship of Lord Bullock* (London: HMSO).

Dewey, J. (1916), *Democracy and Education* (New York: Macmillan).

Doyle, J. F. (ed.) (1973), *Educational Judgments* (London: Routledge & Kegan Paul).

Duane, M. (1971), 'Freedom and the state system of education', in Adams *et al.*, 1971, pp. 180–240.

Entwistle, H. (1971), *Political Education in a Democracy* (London: Routledge & Kegan Paul).

Friedman, M. (1962), *Capitalism and Freedom* (Chicago: University of Chicago Press).

110

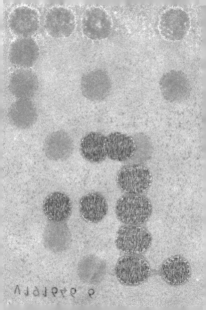

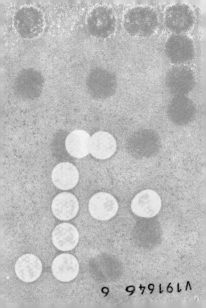

V191646 6

Garforth, F. W. (1962), *Education and Social Purpose* (London: Oldbourne).

Garforth, F. W. (1979), *John Stuart Mill's Theory of Education* (Oxford: Martin Robertson).

Garforth, F. W. (1980), *Educative Democracy* (Oxford: OUP).

Goodman, P. (1971), *Compulsory Miseducation* (Harmondsworth: Penguin).

Greenstein, F. I. (1965), *Children and Politics* (Newhaven, Conn., and London: Yale University Press).

Harré, R., and Secord, P. F. (1972), *The Explanation of Social Behaviour* (Oxford: Blackwell).

Heater, D. (ed.) (1969), *The Teaching of Politics* (London: Methuen).

Heater, D. (1977a), 'Political education in schools: the official attitude', in Crick and Heater, 1977, pp. 27–33.

Heater, D. (1977b), 'Politics as a university discipline and political education in schools', in Crick and Heater, 1977, pp. 51–7.

Hobbes, T. [1651], *Leviathan* (Harmondsworth: Penguin, 1968).

Holt, J. (1977), *Instead of Education* (Harmondsworth: Penguin).

Hook, S. (1963), *Education for Modern Man* (New York: Knopf).

Illich, I. D. (1971), *Deschooling Society* (London: Calder & Boyars).

Jaros, D. (1973), *Socialisation to Politics* (London: Nelson).

Keddie, N. (1971), 'Classroom knowledge', in Young, 1971, pp. 133–60.

Kilpatrick, W. H. (1951), *Philosophy of Education* (New York: Macmillan).

Kingdom, E. (1976), 'Political education' in *Research in Education*, vol. 16, no. 16, pp. 1–12.

Lindsay, A. D. (1929), *The Essentials of Democracy* (London: OUP).

Lister, I. (ed.) (n.d.), *Deschooling: A Reader* (Cambridge: CUP).

Lively, J. (1975), *Democracy* (Oxford: Blackwell).

Lloyd, D. I. (ed.) (1976), *Philosophy and the Teacher* (London: Routledge & Kegan Paul).

Locke, J. [1690], *Two Treatises of Government* (Cambridge: CUP, 1963).

Lucas, J. R. (1976), *Democracy and Participation* (Harmondsworth: Penguin).

Macpherson, C. B. (1966), *The Real World of Democracy* (London: OUP).

Mannheim, K. (1950), *Freedom, Power and Democratic Planning* (London: OUP).

Margolis, M. (1979), *Viable Democracy* (Harmondsworth: Penguin).

Megill, K. A. (1970), *The New Democratic Theory* (New York: The Free Press).

Mill, J. S. (1859), 'On liberty', in Mill, 1910, pp. 65–174.

Mill, J. S. (1861), 'Considerations on representative government', in Mill, 1910, pp. 175–395.

Mill, J. S. (1867), 'Inaugural Address at the University of St. Andrews', in Garforth, 1971, pp. 123–50.

Mill, J. S. (1910), *Utilitarianism, Liberty, Representative Government* (London: Dent).

Neill, A. S. (1962), *Summerhill: A Radical Approach to Education* (London: Gollancz).

Neill, A. S. (1971), 'Freedom works', in Adams *et al.*, 1971, pp. 127–52.

Nelson, W. N. (1980), *On Justifying Democracy* (London: Routledge & Kegan Paul).

Nozick, R. (1974), *Anarchy, State and Utopia* (Oxford: Blackwell).

NUT (National Union of Teachers) (1971), *Teacher Participation: A Study Outline* (London: NUT).

Oakeshott, M. (1962), *Rationalism in Politics* (London: Methuen).

O'Hear, A. (1981), *Education, Society and Human Nature* (London: Routledge & Kegan Paul).

Olafson, F. A. (1973), 'Rights and duties in education', in Doyle, 1973, pp. 173–95.

O'Neill, O., and Ruddick, W. (eds) (1979), *Having Children* (Oxford: OUP).

Pateman, C. (1970), *Participation and Democratic Theory* (Cambridge: CUP).

Peters, R. S. (1966), *Ethics and Education* (London: Allen & Unwin).

Peters, R. S. (1973), 'Freedom and the development of the free man', in Doyle, 1973, pp. 119–42.

Peters, R. S. (1979), 'Democratic values and educational aims', *Teachers College Record*, vol. 80, no. 3, pp. 463–82.

Popper, K. R. (1961), *The Poverty of Historicism* (London: Routledge & Kegan Paul).

Postman, N., and Weingartner, C. (1971), *Teaching as a Subversive Activity* (Harmondsworth: Penguin).

Pring, R. (1975), 'In defence of authority – or how to keep knowledge under control', in Bridges and Scrimshaw, 1975, pp. 20–37.

Rank and File (n.d.), *Democracy in Schools* (London: Rank and File).

Rawls, J. (1972), *A Theory of Justice* (London: OUP).

Reimer, E. (1971), *School Is Dead* (Harmondsworth: Penguin).

Robinson, P. (1981), *Perspectives on the Sociology of Education* (London: Routledge & Kegan Paul).

Rousseau, J. J. [1762], *The Social Contract* (Harmondsworth: Penguin, 1978).

Rubinstein, D., and Stoneman, C. (1970), *Education for Democracy* (Harmondsworth: Penguin).

Schumpeter, J. A. (1954), *Capitalism, Socialism and Democracy* (London: Allen & Unwin).

Scrimshaw, P. (1975), 'Should schools be participant democracies?', in Bridges and Scrimshaw, 1975, pp. 60–80.

Singer, P. (1973), *Democracy and Disobedience* (London: OUP).

Skidelsky, R. (1969), *English Progressive Schools* (Harmondsworth: Penguin).

Smith, C. (1977), *Industrial Participation* (London: McGraw-Hill).

Sockett, H. T. (ed.) (1980), *Accountability in the English Educational System* (London: Hodder & Stoughton).

Stradling, R. (1977), *The Political Awareness of the School Leaver* (London: Hansard Society).

Stradling, R., and Porter, A. (1978), 'Issues and political problems', in Crick and Porter, 1978, pp. 74–81.

Tapper, T., and Salter, B. (1978), *Education and the Political Order* (London: Macmillan).

Ungoed-Thomas, J. R. (1972), *Our School* (London: Longman).

Vaizey, J. (1962), *Education for Tomorrow* (Harmondsworth: Penguin).

Watts, J. (ed.) (1977), *The Countesthorpe Experience* (London: Allen & Unwin).

West, E. C. (1970), *Education and the State* (London: Institute of Economic Affairs).

White, J. (1970), 'Indoctrination: a reply to I. M. M. Gregory and R. G. Woods', *Proceedings of the Philosophy of Education Society of Great Britain*, vol. 4, pp. 107–20.

White, J. (1973), *Towards a Compulsory Curriculum* (London: Routledge & Kegan Paul).

White, J., and White, P. (1980), 'David Cooper's illusions', *Journal of Philosophy of Education*, vol. 14, no. 2, pp. 239–48.

White, J., *et al.* (1981), *No, Minister: A Critique of the DES Paper 'The School Curriculum'* (London: University of London Institute of Education).

White, P. (1971), 'Education, democracy and the public interest', *Proceedings of the Philosophy of Education Society of Great Britain*, vol. 5, no. 1, pp. 7–28.

White, P. (1979), 'Work-place democracy and political education', *Journal of Philosophy of Education*, vol. 13, no. 1, pp. 5–20.

Whitty, G. (1978), 'Political education in schools', *Socialism and Education*, vol. 5, no. 5.

Williams, B., and Montefiore, A. (eds) (1966), *British Analytical Philosophy* (London: Routledge & Kegan Paul).

Wilson, B. (ed.) (1975), *Education, Equality and Society* (London: Allen & Unwin).

Wilson, J., and Cowell, B. (1983), 'The democratic myth', *Journal of Philosophy of Education*, vol. 17, no. 1, pp. 111–17.

Winch, P. (1958), *The Idea of a Social Science* (London: Routledge & Kegan Paul).

Wollheim, R. (1966), 'On the theory of democracy', in Williams and Montefiore, 1966, pp. 247–66.

Wringe, C. A. (1981), *Children's Rights: A Philosophical Study* (London: Routledge & Kegan Paul).

Young, M. F. D. (1971), *Knowledge and Control* (London: Collier Macmillan).

# Index